THREE DIALOGUES
BETWEEN HYLAS
AND PHILONOUS

The Library of Liberal Arts
OSKAR PIEST, FOUNDER

THREE DIALOGUES BETWEEN HYLAS AND PHILONOUS

GEORGE BERKELEY

Edited, with an introduction, by
COLIN M. TURBAYNE

· ·

The Library of Liberal Arts
published by

THE BOBBS-MERRILL COMPANY, INC.
INDIANAPOLIS · NEW YORK

George Berkeley: 1685-1753

THREE DIALOGUES BETWEEN HYLAS AND PHILONOUS
was originally published in 1713

. . . .

CONTENTS

THREE DIALOGUES
BETWEEN HYLAS AND PHILONOUS

CHRONOLOGY

1685 George Berkeley born at Kilkenny, March 12

1696 Entered Kilkenny College

1700 Entered Trinity College, Dublin

1704 Received baccalaureate degree

1707 Junior Fellow; M.A.

1709 Ordained deacon; librarian

1710 Ordained priest; Junior Dean

1712 Junior Greek Lecturer

1713 To London; went to Italy, October

1714 Returned to England

1721 To Dublin; took degrees of B.D. and D.D.; appointed Divinity Lecturer

1722 Appointed Senior Proctor; presented by the Crown to the deanery of Dromore, but the Crown's right to appoint challenged by the Bishop; to London

1723 Returned to Dublin; appointed Hebrew Lecturer; executor and legatee of Hester Van Homrigh

1724 Resigned from Trinity College to become Dean of Derry; to London to raise funds for Bermuda project and get Royal Charter

1726 House of Commons voted a grant for St. Paul's College, Bermuda

1728 Married Anne Forster; sailed for America

1729 Arrived Newport

1731 Left for England

1732 Nominated Dean of Down, but not appointed

1734 Bishop of Cloyne

1741 Declined offer of nomination for Vice-Chancellorship of Dublin University

1745 Declined offer of Bishopric of Clogher

1752 To Oxford

1753 Died, January 14; interred in the Chapel of Christ Church, Oxford

EDITOR'S INTRODUCTION

I

The *Three Dialogues* records an imaginary discussion on the subject of materialism. This discussion occurs in the early mornings of three successive days in the garden of an unknown college. The speakers are Hylas, a "materialist," and Philonous, an immaterialist who represents Berkeley. Both are educated men and Christians. They share the view that the immediate objects of perception are ideas which exist only in the mind. Hylas holds that all of these ideas are the effects, while some are the resemblances, of material entities which cannot be perceived by human minds and are real things. Philonous, who was once a "materialist," denies the existence of such material entities and holds that the things immediately perceived are the real things. These things (ideas or collections of them) are sometimes perceived by us and are always perceived by God who causes them. By the end of the First Dialogue, Hylas, if not convinced that matter does not exist, is at least silenced. At the end of the Second, he has been reduced to a state of skepticism. At the conclusion of the discussion, Hylas has been converted to immaterialism.

Berkeley brought the manuscript of the *Dialogues* with him to London in January, 1713. Three years earlier he had published in Dublin *The Principles of Human Knowledge*. It had been most unfavorably received. In London, particularly, it had been immediately ridiculed. A physician argued that its author must be mad. A bishop pitied Berkeley for seeking notoriety by trying to start something new. A third critic said that Berkeley was not as far gone as another thinker who denied not only the existence of matter, but of persons. Many factors may have led to the failure of the *Principles*. To read it through required a great deal of intellectual effort. Moreover, the paradox that matter does not exist, which Berkeley advanced, was a bold one. In all ages people are prone to regard oddness as a test of truth. Again, the terms "matter" and "idea," which Berkeley constantly used, are ambiguous. Most people use the word "matter" to refer to common things, not to material substance. The word "idea" is customarily used to refer to images or thoughts and not to common things. Finally, the *Principles* had not been published in London. Berkeley, it seems, became aware of all these factors and acted on them. He proceeded to cast his notions into dramatic form, using Plato's dialogues as his model. He wrote in "the most easy and familiar manner." He weeded out as much as possible of the philosophers' jargon and took pains to explain the use of those technical terms he had to keep. He eliminated much technical detail. Once again he raised all the objections to his views he could think of. Although he wrote, this time, mainly for the vulgar or common man, and not for the philosophers, he constantly observed the most rigid rules of reasoning. He used all his skill to show that his views were closer to common sense than were those of the philosophers which he opposed. The result was a combination of philosophical insight and literary art not yet surpassed. The *Three Dialogues* was published in London in May, 1713, and was barely noticed. A reprint appeared in 1725 and a new edition in 1734, the last in Berkeley's lifetime.

II

Berkeley tells us in the Preface that the *Principles* had the same design as the *Dialogues*. In the latter he merely intends "to treat more clearly and fully of certain principles laid down" in the former, and "to place them in a new light." The reader is not required to know the contents of the earlier work. The design is to divert the mind of man from "vain researches" by inquiring into "the source of its perplexities." He does not tell us in the Preface, probably out of prudence, that he considers the source of the mind's perplexities to be the belief in the existence of matter or material substance.

Following this, his design is to lay down principles which will rescue the mind of man from those "endless pursuits" which occupy it, and finally, to provide a "plain demonstration" of the immediate providence of God.

This design subserves a wider purpose. Berkeley holds that the end of speculation is practice. Accordingly, these books are to prepare men's minds for the study and practice of virtue. The *Principles* was the first part of a plan which included at least a second part on psychology and ethics, a third on physics, and probably a fourth on mathematics. None of the later parts was published, although the bulk of the second was written and then lost during Berkeley's travels.

However, although these two books have avowedly the same design, there is a striking difference of emphasis in the *Dialogues*. In the *Principles,* Berkeley had, in the main, directed his arguments against the views of the philosophers, but he had nevertheless sided with the philosophers against some common sense views. He had not courted the common man but he had not expected his own views to be so misinterpreted as to have ascribed to him the denial of the reality of sensible things. In the *Dialogues,* Berkeley is concerned, not only to deny the philosophers' belief in the existence of matter—an attitude implicit or explicit in the views of the mathematicians, physicists and metaphysicians of that day—but to declare that his own doctrine is on the side of common sense and religion. He thinks that there is no real controversy between his views and those of the vulgar. Hylas promises to embrace that opinion "most agreeable to common sense, and remote from skepticism" (p. 108). This book accordingly might have had as its subtitle: "A vindication of common sense against the innovations of the philosophers." But Berkeley's position does not seem to be, at first, consonant with the universal sense of mankind. This has to be shown. He admits that he must use "some ambages and ways of speech not common" (p. 92), but asserts that however oddly his view that "there is nothing in the world but spirits and ideas . . . may sound in words, yet it includes nothing so very strange or shocking in its sense, which in effect amounts to no more than this, to wit, that there are only things perceiving and things perceived" (pp. 82f.).

Thus, in the *Dialogues* Berkeley sets himself two things: first, to refute "materialism," that is, to prove that material substance does not exist; and secondly, to show that his position is more agreeable to the common sense of mankind and to religion. So Hylas is taken on a tour through the "wild mazes of philosophy" beginning with premises accepted by philosophers and ending with a view opposed to theirs and agreeable to that of the vulgar. He is conducted by an expert who asks only that reason and attention replace prejudice and authority.

III

The nature of the materialism which Berkeley seeks to refute is illuminated by comparing it with the view of the common man. Berkeley thinks that according to common sense real things can be immediately perceived, that these things exist independently of any human mind. He also thinks that the common man believes in God who is constantly aware of these real things. The word "matter," he holds, is "never used by common people, or if ever, it is to signify the immediate objects of sense" (p. 111). In the language of the philosophers, the common man, according to Berkeley, would hold that the primary qualities of bodies such as size, shape, position, and movement, as well as the secondary qualities, such as color, sound, and smell, can be perceived immediately and exist while unperceived by human minds.

The philosophers, according to Berkeley, are sharply opposed to common sense. They hold that material substance exists, although it cannot be perceived. It requires nothing beyond itself in order to exist. Matter or its unperceived qualities, such as size, shape, etc., can cause ideas in our minds which resemble the primary qualities. In addition it has secondary qualities which are merely powers producing ideas in us such as colors, sounds, etc. There is nothing like these ideas of secondary qualities in matter. Thus, as Berkeley uses it, the term "materialism" has a wider meaning than the more common one, which is the doctrine that nothing exists except matter and its movements and modifications. According to Berkeley, a materialist may hold that mind or spiritual substance exists.

These views of the philosophers, according to Berkeley, lead to other erroneous and absurd views. First, he saw that belief in the existence of matter, as described above, entails skepticism: the things we perceive are not real things but only images of them. Thus there is knowledge only if the representations are true. But since the originals are unknown, it is impossible to know whether our ideas are images. Therefore, we cannot know whether our knowledge is real, and "we are thrown into the most hopeless and abandoned skepticism" (p. 94). Secondly, he saw that belief in matter is the source of paradoxes and perplexities: "That the qualities we perceive are not on the objects, that we must not believe our senses, that we know nothing of the real nature of things . . . that real colors and sounds are nothing but certain unknown figures and motions (p. 91) . . . (that) two independent substances, so widely different as *spirit* and *matter,* should mutually operate on each other" (p. 107). Thirdly, he saw that belief in the absolute existence of material substance with its attendant absolute space and absolute motion leads people to give metaphysical validity to physical or mechanical explanations. Berkeley approved of the great physical discoveries of the seventeenth century, but he saw that they demanded an adequate philosophy of science and a true metaphysics. Galileo's first law of motion, it seemed, removed the necessity of a spiritual force to keep bodies moving, for the simple reason that no force is required. Newton's law of gravitation appeared to save all the phenomena connected with the revolution of celestial bodies except for some observed irregularities.

Scientific advances may be irrelevant to the question of God's existence; Newton thought they were an additional demonstration; but Berkeley could see the effect on peoples' minds of the success of physical explanations. If they are treated as ultimately true, God becomes either very remote or unnecessary. Berkeley contrasts the effect on men's minds of "the apprehension of a distant Deity" with that of the awareness of God's immediate presence (p. 107).

According to Berkeley then, belief in material substance is the main source of our confusions. Immaterialism, as its name implies, is a dissentient doctrine. If he can prove that matter does not exist, he thinks he will have removed the main support of skepticism, eliminated many paradoxes, cleared the way for restoring to men's minds belief in the immediate presence of God, and brought men back to common sense.

The arguments Berkeley used against materialism may be reduced to two kinds: those in which he tried to show that material substance has no real existence; and those in which he tried to show that matter is a useless working hypothesis, that is, considered as a causal explanation, it fails to explain. The argument on which he set most store belongs to the first kind. Its predominant characteristic is Berkeley's use of the key relation of *resemblance* or *similarity*. The arguments of the second kind are characterized by the relation of *causality*. These two relations are the essential relations of the materialist position. For the materialist, the terms of each relation are material entities and ideas. For Berkeley, they turn out to be, on the one hand, ideas and other ideas, and on the other hand, God and ideas. The first kind of argument against materialism is to be found in the First Dialogue. The second occurs in the Second Dialogue. In the Third Dialogue, Berkeley meets numerous objections to his own position which has emerged from his denial of matter; and it is mainly in this last dialogue that Berkeley develops a third kind of argument to the conclusion that immaterialism is agreeable to common sense. I shall present these three kinds of arguments, in the order given above, in the three following sections.

IV

The chief features of the materialism which Berkeley sought to refute have been outlined. There are, however, variations of the doctrine, of which Berkeley was aware. Two main versions are distinguishable. They may conveniently be described in their relation to the distinction between primary and secondary qualities. According to the first version (p. 28, also *Principles* §10), the primary qualities, such as extension, figure, and motion, inhere in external bodies, but we are able to perceive these qualities directly. The secondary qualities, such as colors, tastes, and sounds, are asserted to be ideas or sensations which exist only in our minds. According to the second version of the main doctrine (pp. 19, 21, 27, 48, also *Principles* §9) neither the primary nor the secondary qualities are perceivable. All we perceive are ideas *of* these qualities. Our ideas of the primary qualities are exact resemblances of them. Our ideas of the secondary qualities represent them but resemble nothing in external bodies. The secondary qualities are powers depending on the primary qualities, which cause in our minds ideas of colors, tastes, etc. Both these versions of the main materialist doctrine are found in the philosophy of Locke. The second is avowedly his official position, but he often writes as though he subscribes to the first.

These versions of the materialist doctrine which had been held by Berkeley's precursors must be distinguished, otherwise some of Berkeley's arguments may seem to be misdirected. Berkeley's arguments of the first kind are, chiefly, three arguments, two subordinate and the third which must, I think, be considered as his main argument against materialism. The subordinate arguments are the argument from the relativity of all sensible qualities and the argument from the impossibility of abstracting certain qualities from others. The former begins by showing that since the secondary qualities vary in relation to the perceiver they cannot be in external objects (pp. 18-28). Then it proceeds to show that similar considerations apply to the primary qualities (pp. 28-32). This argument had already been advanced by Berkeley's great precursor, Bayle. Similar arguments are as old as the Sophists. Since it assumes that all the qualities of bodies are perceivable, it can be directed only against the first version of materialism outlined in the preceding paragraph. Even then, as Berkeley noted in the *Principles* (§15), it shows only that we do not know through sense the real qualities of bodies. Hence, it is difficult to understand why Berkeley gives the bulk of the *First Dialogue* to it. The second subordinate argument which Berkeley uses, and which seems to be his own, purports to show that the primary and secondary qualities are united and in the mind, because it is impossible to abstract, e.g., extension or motion from color, either in perception or imagination (p. 34 and *Principles* §10). Since this argument assumes that both the primary and secondary qualities can be perceived and imagined and that the latter are in the mind, it may succeed only against the first version of materialism.

Neither of the above subordinate arguments can possibly succeed against the second version of materialism, which is Locke's official position, because they do not affect the supposedly unperceivable qualities of bodies. In terms then of the doctrine that all we perceive are ideas *of* primary and secondary qualities, the two preceding arguments can at most confirm that all our ideas are in our minds. They cannot show that the material entities, supposed to underlie the things we perceive, are ideas. In terms of Malebranche's distinction (more or less acceptable to many modern philosophers such as Russell and Eddington) between physical space and perceptual space, these arguments do not prove that the inferred unperceived physical objects in physical space are either perceivable or nonexistent.

Berkeley's main argument against materialism had been used repeatedly by him in the *Principles*. In the *Dialogues*, Berkeley, like his model Plato, a master of dramatic suspense, keeps this argument in reserve until the close of the First Dialogue (pp. 45-49). Hylas presents the doctrine of the materialists, acceptable to such philosophers as Locke, Malebranche, and Des-

our ideas. For example, while the primary qualities of extension and motion turn out to be ideas, the secondary qualities corresponding to our ideas of color and sound do not. In other words, this argument may succeed against that moderate version of the materialist doctrine which asserts that all qualities are perceivable and that secondary qualities are ideas, but it only partially succeeds against the more extreme version, that is, Locke's official doctrine.

That Berkeley intends his argument to be directed against both the moderate and extreme versions of the materialist doctrine may be seen from a careful reading of the *Principles* (§§7-9) and the *Dialogues* (pp. 45-49). In answer to the above objection, the following considerations are relevant: (1) if the secondary qualities are ideas, as some materialists admit, the argument shows that the primary and secondary qualities are united, and in the mind; (2) if the ideas *of* secondary qualities do not resemble the secondary qualities of bodies, that is, if they have no archetypes, then the secondary qualities as archetypes do not exist, and no proof is required that there are none (*Principles,* §9); (3) if the secondary qualities are causes of our ideas in the form of "powers" dependent on the primary qualities, then, since the primary qualities have been shown to be ideas, the former lack causal efficacy, as Berkeley tries to show elsewhere; (4) if our ideas are held to be caused by material entities of any kind, then this view is the subject of Berkeley's second type of argument, to be presented in the next section; (5) the above objection, if sustained, does not affect the main conclusion of the argument, which is that matter as defined by its primary qualities is impossible.

The major premise and the conclusion of what I have called "The Berkeleian Syllogism" had been conjoined by Berkeley when he was forming his philosophy while writing the *Philosophical Commentaries* to make: The Principle, i.e., that neither our ideas nor anything like our ideas can possibly be in an unperceiving thing (entry 379). Berkeley employs the Principle repeatedly throughout his major works.[3] It is dis-

---

[3] *Principles,* §§22, 45, 47; *Dialogues,* pp. 30, 56, 94.

tinct from, and of a lower order than, his Axiom: *esse* is *percipi* or *percipere,* which is Berkeley's highest metaphysical principle, constituting a concise reference to all there is. Berkeley's main argument against materialism which we have been considering was discovered by him when he was twenty-two years old. It was the supreme insight of his life, the turning point in his philosophical development, in which "ye immaterial hypothesis" became "the Principle."

V

Berkeley's second main kind of argument is directed against the view that material substance is the cause of our ideas. Hylas presents the basic elements of this view:

I find myself affected with various ideas, whereof I know I am not the cause; neither are they the cause of themselves. . . . They have, therefore, some cause distinct from me and them, of which I pretend to know no more than that it is *the cause of my ideas.* And this thing, whatever it be, I call "matter" (p. 60).

Hylas presents in the Second Dialogue various modifications of this view. Matter is put forward as a probable hypothesis as a way of explaining or of "accounting for our sensations or ideas" (p. 51). It is a cause subordinate to God which "concurs in the production of our ideas . . . by that kind of action which belongs to matter, *viz.* motion" (p. 61); or it is an "instrument" (p. 62), or an "occasion" (p. 64). Finally, it is supposed to explain the reality of things (p. 69).

Against this view on the causation of our ideas Berkeley's argument has three parts. In the first, he finds that matter is an inadequate scientific hypothesis; in the second, he shows that certain entities, later called by him "mathematical hypotheses," do not exist in nature; in the third, he finds that the materialists confuse physical with metaphysical causes. The first two parts are only barely developed in the *Dialogues,* whereas the third is fully presented. They are included in Berkeley's philosophy of science and are amplified in *De Motu* and *Siris.* In order to clarify Berkeley's account, I shall draw

on these works mainly for terminology, for, although it undergoes some development, his view is implicit in the *Dialogues*.

Hylas, after partial conversion, asserts: " 'Material substance' was no more than a hypothesis, and a false and groundless one too" (p. 75). This assertion characterizes the first part of Berkeley's argument. Berkeley distinguishes between laws of nature or principles, such as Newton's law of gravitation, and mathematical hypotheses, or devices or phantoms. Some of the latter, in Berkeley's opinion, are useful; some are useless. He writes of "absolute space, that phantom of the mechanic and geometrical philosophers," [4] and he asserts: "To throw light on nature it is idle to adduce things which are neither evident to the senses, nor intelligible to reason." [5] Thus, while attraction and gravity are useful mathematical hypotheses, absolute space and absolute motion are not. Berkeley evidently regards matter as a useless mathematical hypothesis, for Philonous asserts:

Now, if you can prove that any philosopher has explained the production of any one idea in our minds by the help of *matter*, I shall for ever acquiesce and look on all that has been said against it as nothing (p. 90);

and again:

. . . I challenge you to show me that thing in nature which needs matter to explain or account for it (p. 69).

Berkeley's doctrine on the ontological status of mathematical hypotheses in general, and on matter in particular, is revealed in Philonous' remark: "matter . . . can have no more claim to existence than a golden mountain or a centaur" (p. 70). He enlarges on this when, in *De Motu*, he says that Newton introduced attraction, "not as a true, physical quality, but only as a mathematical hypothesis." [6] In *Siris*, after praising Newton's mechanics, he suggests that Newton tends "to forget himself in his manner of speaking of physical agents

[4] *Siris*, §271.
[5] *De Motu*, §21.
[6] §17.

. . . and in supposing real forces to exist in bodies . . .[7]
Berkeley's reasons for the above conclusion on the nonexistence of matter as an instance of a mathematical hypothesis are
obvious. Philonous shows (pp. 66-70) that matter like the
golden mountain cannot be given a location; it cannot be perceived or inferred; like all mathematical hypotheses, the word
"matter" designates nothing (p. 68).

The last part of Berkeley's argument against matter as the
cause of our ideas is his doctrine that the ultimate explanation
of the production and of the continued existence of our ideas
is an infinite mind. A cause for Berkeley must be an efficient
active cause. Ideas or collections of ideas are passive, inert
things which are effects. Matter, as defined by the materialists,
is inert, and so can produce nothing. In the Second Dialogue
Berkeley presents his own two arguments for the existence of
God. One of them, based on Berkeley's Principle, is an argument unique in natural theology. The other is a variant of
the cosmological argument. These two arguments correspond
to, and incorporate Berkeley's positive addition to, his arguments against matter as *cause*. His first proof of God's existence is:

> The sensible world exists if, and only if, it is
>   perceived by a mind;
> The sensible world exists unperceived by human
>   minds;
> Therefore, the sensible world must be perceived
>   by an infinite mind.

Berkeley's second proof begins with the first premise above
and continues: "These ideas or things by me perceived, either
themselves or their archetypes, exist independently of my
mind; since I know myself not to be their author . . . They
must, therefore, exist in some other mind, whose will it is they
should be exhibited to me" (p. 58).

At first glance it might be thought that Berkeley in the
Dialogues is completely opposed to second corporeal causes
and physical explanations. However, his mature view of *De*

7 §246.

Motu and *Siris* is implicit and partially explicit. This is that physical explanations are compatible with metaphysical ones; that it is illegitimate to hold that physical explanations are either sufficient to account for phenomena or that they deal with a world of occult forces behind phenomena; that it is not the business of physics to establish efficient causes; but that "by observing and reasoning upon the connection of ideas, they (the physicists) discover the laws and methods of nature" (p. 90). Within this framework it is legitimate to speak of "second corporeal causes" [8] and to speak as Berkeley himself does, in *Siris,* as follows: "Nature seems better known and explained by attractions and repulsions than by those other mechanical principles of size, figure and the like; that is, by Sir Isaac Newton, than Descartes." [9]

VI

At the beginning of the Third Dialogue, Hylas is in a sorry plight. He admits he has relinquished his belief in the existence of material substance. This belief had been as secure as any. Accordingly, all his other beliefs are rendered vain and uncertain. From this state of doubt he plunges even deeper. He agrees with Philonous that all we can perceive are our own ideas or appearances and that these exist only in the mind. But from this he infers that we cannot know whether any real thing exists in nature or what its true nature is. He goes further and declares that it is impossible for any "real corporeal thing" to exist.

Philonous quickly diagnoses Hylas' ailment as "the deepest and most deplorable skepticism that ever man was (in)," because Hylas does more than doubt, he denies "the real existence of any part of the universe" (p. 75). Then Philonous names the source of his ailment: It is Hylas' previous belief in matter, which makes him "dream" of these unknown natures in everything and which makes him distinguish between real things and the appearances of things. Hylas agrees with

[8] See also Plato *Timaeus,* 46c, 68c. Cf. *Timaeus* (Jowett), ed. by Glenn R. Morrow ("The Library of Liberal Arts" No. 14), pp. 28 and 51f., resp.
[9] §243.

this diagnosis, but quickly retorts that any theory of reality, including Philonous' own, must lead inevitably to skepticism when analyzed. He begs leave to become the interrogator in order to demonstrate this. Before this can occur, Philonous administers his cure.

He begins by asserting, without any attempt at a formal demonstration, that he sides with common sense: "I am of a vulgar cast, simple enough to believe my senses, and leave things as I find them" (p. 76). Then he proceeds to demonstrate one important aspect of immaterialism:

Wood, stones, fire, water, flesh, iron, and the like things which I name and discourse of are things that I know. And I should not have known them, but that I perceived them by my senses; and things perceived by the senses are immediately perceived; and things immediately perceived are ideas; and ideas cannot exist without the mind; their existence therefore consists in being perceived; when therefore they are actually perceived, there can be no doubt of their existence (p. 76).

This argument, which proves that the *esse* of sensible things is *percipi*, is Berkeley's formal attempt to unite immaterialism with common sense. It is Berkeley's way of assimilating two important notions held by the vulgar and the philosophers: "the former being of opinion that *those things they immediately perceive are the real things,* and the latter, that *the things immediately perceived are ideas which exist only in the mind*" (p. 112). Moreover it refutes the skepticism into which it appears one must be plunged after denying the existence of matter. It does this in a most ingenious yet simple way, by accepting the skeptical conclusion of one such as Hylas that all we can ever know of the external world are certain ideas or appearances, and then admitting, as any consistent empiricist must, that these appearances are real.[10] After all,

[10] Richard H. Popkin in "Berkeley and Pyrrhonism," *The Review of Metaphysics,* Vol. V, No. 2, December 1951, writes: "Only Berkeley with his insistence that the world of appearance is the real world could defend common sense realism and challenge Pyrrhonism on its own battlefield, the world of sensible things. Only Berkeley could accept the skeptical arguments and not their nihilistic conclusions and thus overcome 'la crise pyrrhonienne'."

it is ridiculous to hold, as do the materialists whom Berkeley is attacking, that the things we see and touch are illusions. Berkeley, the empiricist, makes Philonous exclaim: "What a jest it is for a philosopher to question the existence of sensible things . . . ," (pp. 76f.) [11] and again, "We both, therefore, agree in this, that we perceive only sensible forms; but herein we differ: you will have them to be empty appearances, I real beings. In short, you do not trust your senses, I do" (p. 92). The above argument proves what is sometimes known as Berkeley's "phenomenalism" if it is allowed that ideas or appearances may be collected into bundles, that is, if the premise "the things perceived are ideas," which Berkeley takes from the philosophers and makes his own, may be read as "the things perceived are ideas or collections of ideas." Berkeley writes: "A cherry, I say, is nothing but a congeries of sensible impressions, or ideas perceived by various senses, which ideas are united into one thing (or have one name given them) by the mind" (p. 97).

With this argument, Berkeley has largely completed his design. He has proved, to his satisfaction, immaterialism. Corresponding to the three main arguments which I have presented, immaterialism emerges as the threefold doctrine: first, that material substance has no real existence; secondly, that God, and not matter, is the efficient cause of our ideas, and thirdly, that our ideas are real things. It follows, if Berkeley's arguments are sound, that two kinds of things exist in the universe. Both can be known. They are things perceiving and things perceived, or minds and their ideas. From the

11 Seen in this light, both Dr. Johnson's notorious ostensive refutation of Berkeley's "ingenious sophistry," by exclaiming while "striking his foot with mighty force against a large stone, till he rebounded from it, 'I refute it *thus*'," and G. E. Moore's celebrated proof of an external world, "By holding up my two hands, and saying, as I make a certain gesture with the right hand, 'Here is one hand,' and adding, as I make a certain gesture with the left, 'and here is another'," are vindications of Berkeley. See *Life of Johnson* (Globe Edition, Macmillan, London, 1929), p. 162; and G. E. Moore, "Proof of an External World," *Proceedings of the British Academy*, Vol. 25, 1939, p. 295.

denial of matter has flowed the denial of atheism and skepticism, which have been replaced by the immediate presence of an infinite mind and by the reality of knowledge.

In his efforts to vindicate common sense against the innovations of the philosophers, Berkeley has been forced to violate some of the canons of common English usage. His most violent infringement is his strange use of the word "idea." Since some critics have objected to Berkeley's use of an ordinary word in an extraordinary sense, since Berkeley has done so deliberately, since it is the key word in his system, and since to understand how Berkeley uses it is to understand Berkeley, it is necessary to note some of the important features of Berkeley's use of this word.

Berkeley uses the word "idea" ambiguously, but whether he equivocates is doubtful. He chose the term not only because it was fashionable in the new philosophy, but out of convenience. Moreover, he accepts the premises of his opponents which contain it. The last utterance of Hylas in the *Dialogues* begins: "You set out upon the same principles that Academics, Cartesians, and the like sects usually do . . ." These principles reduce to two: *The objects immediately perceived are ideas;* and: *All ideas exist in the mind.* On these propositions, held on all sides to be self-evident, Berkeley builds his system. Clearly he intends to use the word "idea" in the above premises in the same sense that the philosophers use it, to refer to the immediate data of sense, memory, or imagination. It is therefore obvious that at this stage both Berkeley and the philosophers would agree that the *esse* of ideas of sense is *percipi*. No claim is made here that these ideas are real or permanent. They are phantasms, as fleeting as dreams, utterly dependent on human perceivers for their existence.

In the next stage, the denotation of the word increases enormously. Berkeley diverges from the materialists like Locke, Malebranche, Descartes, Hobbes, Galileo, and Boyle, but not from the skeptics like Bayle, Fardella, *et. al.* As a result of his main argument against matter (presented above, sec. IV) in which the crucial premise was "All things like ideas are ideas,"

the originals or archetypes of our ideas, if they can be perceived, are found to be other ideas, and if not, nonexistent.
Since these archetypes are the so-called primary qualities of
bodies, the skeptics, but not the materialists, would undoubtedly share Berkeley's view that the *esse* of the primary qualities of bodies is *percipi*. As before, no claim need be made
that ideas are permanent or real. They are phantasms, having
the same ontological status as the ideas of Locke and the
Cartesians. All that has occurred is a notable increase in the
denotation of the term. It still may mean what Locke means
by it, the immediate object of perception or thought. This is
the stage reached by the skeptical Hylas at the beginning of
the third dialogue when he asserts that all is mere appearance
or idea. It is the stage from which Hylas thinks Philonous
himself has no escape, when the former asserts: ". . . you leave
us nothing but the empty forms of things, the outside only
which strikes the senses" (p. 92).

The final stage in the development of the term "idea" is
characterized by Philonous' remark: "I am not for changing
things into ideas but rather ideas into things" (p. 92). This
stage is reached by the two remaining main arguments. As a
result of Berkeley's proof of the existence of God, ideas receive
the permanence which, according to common sense, the ordinary things we see and touch must have. Attending this proof
is Berkeley's distinction between ideas of sense and ideas of
imagination, the former being independent of our will. This
property is necessary to a common thing, distinguishing it
from a chimera (p. 82). Berkeley's last main argument which
unites ideas with common things completes the process. As
a result of these arguments, the term "idea" may refer to the
ordinary things of our daily lives which do not cease to exist
when we turn our backs or go to sleep. Ideas now have all
the reality or permanence which we require of common things.
Berkeley has left both the materialists and the skeptics far
behind when he holds that the *esse* of common things is *percipi,* but it must be noticed that *percipi* is now ambiguous,
referring, according to context, to the awareness of God or
man.

VII

In the Third Dialogue, Hylas submits Philonous to such an extensive and searching interrogation that the objections he raises to immaterialism almost exhaust the long list of those raised against Berkeley since 1713. So prescient was Berkeley that most of the objections raised by such well-known figures in the eighteenth century, as Leibniz, Reid, Hume, Dr. Johnson, and Kant, and, in the twentieth, by Russell, Moore, and Ryle, are included.

One finds here the following commonly raised objections: that Berkeley denies the existence of the corporeal world; that things cease to exist when unperceived; that if the arguments against matter are valid, the same may be used against mind; that the self is only a system of floating ideas; that the denial of matter is novel, odd, and shocking; that Berkeley misuses ordinary language; that immaterialism fails to distinguish between real things and ideas; that it fails to provide an adequate explanation of the fact of illusion; that to deny physical causes is extravagant; that no two people can see the same thing, which is absurd; that there is no room in the mind for trees and houses; and that immaterialism is inconsistent with the scriptural account of creation.

Berkeley's defense against these objections is a masterpiece of dialectic. While he is always able to show that immaterialism provides an adequate solution to all the difficulties raised, three features of method dominate his defense: first, he is often able to show either that his doctrine can provide a better explanation or that the objection can be redirected against materialism. This feature is manifested in his answer to the objection that immaterialism cannot explain illusions of sense, since, according to Berkeley, men judge of the reality of things by their senses. This objection vanishes when Berkeley indicates that such appearances as the change of colors in a pigeon's neck, the crooked oar in the water, the round tower, or the moon seen as only a foot in diameter are real and that error lies, not in our experience of such things, but in the inferences made from them. In short, there are no sense illusions, only delusions. Once we "but place the reality of things in ideas, fleeting indeed, and changeable; however, not changed at random, but according to the fixed order of nature," the difficulty recedes; but let reality consist in unperceived originals beyond the appearances, and the difficulty remains (pp. 85f., 108).

The second feature is Berkeley's use of the maxim: "That which bears equally hard on two contradictory opinions can be proof against neither" (pp. 97, 109). One important example of its use is in his answer to the objection about identity. On his principles, no two can see the same thing, because all we perceive are our own ideas. Berkeley replies that if the word "same" is used as it commonly is, to apply to things where there is no perceived difference, then two people may see the same thing. If it is used in the sense of the philosophers who have an abstract idea of identity, defined in various ways, then the matter is one of controversy. Moreover, the philosophers themselves acknowledge that all we perceive are our own ideas. The difficulty, therefore, bears equally hard on both sides, and the objection cannot be sustained against Berkeley.

The third feature is the most striking. Berkeley is able to show that most of the objections are instances of *mistaking the question,* that is, they commit "that vulgar sophism," *ignoratio elenchi.* Two objections have been raised against Berkeley more often than any others. It is held that he denies the existence of the corporeal world, and that according to his principles things cease to exist when unperceived. This is a strange judgment which posterity has made upon a man who was at great pains to make his meaning clear. Berkeley does deny the real existence of the "unknown somewhat" which is supposed to underlie the things we see and which cannot be perceived; "but if by 'material substance' is meant only sensible body, that which is seen and felt" (pp. 84f.), Berkeley asserts a view which the materialists deny. Regarding the second of these two objections, the difference between Berkeley and his objectors is again a verbal one. He agrees with the common man that things continue to exist while unperceived by human beings; but since the common man is assuredly not an atheist, Berkeley is able to maintain that he and the common man agree that things are always perceived by an infinite mind. Berkeley merely adds to this belief that they *are,* perceived his unique doctrine that they *must be* perceived.

The objections and their answers in the third dialogue greatly clarify Berkeley's meaning. One passage shows once and for all where Berkeley draws the line between existence and nonexistence:

Many things, for aught I know, may exist, whereof neither I nor any other man has or can have any idea or notion whatsoever. But then those things must be possible, that is, nothing inconsistent must be included in their definition (p. 79).

The line is clearly drawn between two groups. In the first are real things, such as the motion of the earth (p. 86), and "innumerable worlds revolving round the central fires," so "far sunk in the abyss of space" as to lie quite beyond the reach of telescopes or even the imagination (p. 54). In the second are supposed entities which are impossible, but for which we have words, such as "entity in general" (p. 67) or "material substance" (p. 70).

Although Hylas predicts that "men will come into your notions with small difficulty," Berkeley has had few followers. He is, however, being increasingly read. He is one of the most appealing of philosophers. The *Three Dialogues* presents, in short space, his whole system. It is an admirable introduction to Berkeley and to philosophy.

COLIN M. TURBAYNE

UNIVERSITY OF WASHINGTON
August, 1954

SELECTED BIBLIOGRAPHY

WORKS BY BERKELEY

Philosophical Commentaries. Notes written 1707-08. First published by A. C. Fraser, 1871. This title given by A. A. Luce ed. London, 1944.

An Essay towards a New Theory of Vision, 1709.

A Treatise concerning the Principles of Human Knowledge, Part I, 1710.

Passive Obedience, 1712.

Three Dialogues between Hylas and Philonous, 1713.

De Motu, 1721.

Alciphron: or the Minute Philosopher, 1732.

The Theory of Vision Vindicated and Explained, 1733.

The Analyst, 1734.

The Querist, 1735-7.

Siris, 1744.

The Works of George Berkeley, Bishop of Cloyne, ed. by A. A. Luce and T. E. Jessop, eds., 9 vols. Vols. I-VI, Edinburgh, 1948-54.

WORKS ABOUT BERKELEY

Adamson, R., "Berkeley" in *Encyclopedia Britannica,* Edinburgh, 9th ed., 1875, 11th ed., 1910.

Balfour, A. J., "Biographical Introduction" in *The Works of George Berkeley, Bishop of Cloyne,* ed. by George Sampson, London, 1897.

Fraser, A. C., *Berkeley,* Edinburgh, 1881.

Hicks, G. Dawes, *Berkeley,* London, 1932.

Johnston, G. A., *The Development of Berkeley's Philosophy,* London, 1923.

Luce, A. A., *Berkeley and Malebranche*, Oxford, 1934.

———*The Life of George Berkeley, Bishop of Cloyne*, Edinburgh, 1949.

Rand, Benjamin, *Berkeley and Percival*, Cambridge, 1914.

Wild, John, *George Berkeley, A Study of His Life and Philosophy*, Cambridge, 1936.

"George Berkeley Bicentenary," *The British Journal for the Philosophy of Science*, Vol. IV, No. 13, (May, 1953).

Revue internationale de philosophie (1953). Fascicule 1-2, Nos. 23-24.

NOTE ON THE TEXT

The *Three Dialogues* was first published in 1713. On the title page of this edition, Berkeley said his purpose in writing them was "plainly to demonstrate the reality and perfection of human knowledge, the incorporeal nature of the soul, and the immediate providence of a Deity: in opposition to skeptics and atheists; also to open a method for rendering the sciences more easy, useful, and compendious." In 1725, the work was reissued and called the "second edition." A revised edition, Berkeley's final version, appeared in 1734. The text printed here has been thoroughly compared with the edition of 1734, and the main variations from the earlier editions have been noted. These consist of three bracketed additions on pp. 31, 58, and 79, and one deletion on p. 83, l. 16. After "perceptions," the following passage was omitted: "without any regard either to consistency or the old known axiom, *Nothing can give to another that which it has not itself.*" The present edition includes also the Dedication and the Preface, which Berkeley omitted from his final edition.

The editor has added "not" in brackets on p. 91, l. 30, in order to correct an obvious typographical error. Spelling, punctuation, capitalization, and editorial style have been revised to conform to current American usage.

THE PREFACE [1]

THOUGH it seems the general opinion of the world, no less than the design of Nature and Providence, that the end of speculation be practice or the improvement and regulation of our lives and actions; yet those who are most addicted to speculative studies seem as generally of another mind. And, indeed, if we consider the pains that have been taken to perplex the plainest things—that distrust of the senses, those doubts and scruples, those abstractions and refinements that occur in the very entrance of the sciences—it will not seem strange that men of leisure and curiosity should lay themselves out in fruitless disquisitions without descending to the practical parts of life, or informing themselves in the more necessary and important parts of knowledge.

Upon the common principles of philosophers we are not assured of the existence of things from their being perceived. And we are taught to distinguish their real nature from that which falls under our senses. Hence arise skepticism and paradoxes. It is not enough that we see and feel, that we taste and smell a thing: its true nature, its absolute external entity, is still concealed. For, though it be the fiction of our own brain, we have made it inaccessible to all our faculties. Sense is fallacious, reason defective. We spend our lives in doubting of those things which other men evidently know, and believing those things which they laugh at and despise.

In order, therefore, to divert the busy mind of man from vain researches, it seemed necessary to inquire into the source of its perplexities and, if possible, to lay down such principles as, by an easy solution of them, together with their own native evidence, may at once recommend themselves for genuine to

[1] This Preface was omitted by the author in the edition of 1734.

5

the mind, and rescue it from those endless pursuits it is engaged in. Which with a plain demonstration of the immediate providence of an all-seeing God and the natural immortality of the soul should seem the readiest preparation, as well as the strongest motive, to the study and practice of virtue.

This design I proposed in the First Part of a treatise concerning the *Principles of Human Knowledge,* published in the year 1710. But, before I proceed to publish the Second Part, I thought it requisite to treat more clearly and fully of certain principles laid down in the First and to place them in a new light. Which is the business of the following *Dialogues.*

In this treatise, which does not presuppose in the reader any knowledge of what was contained in the former, it has been my aim to introduce the notions I advance into the mind in the most easy and familiar manner, especially because they carry with them a great opposition to the prejudices of philosophers which have so far prevailed against the common sense and natural notions of mankind.

If the principles which I here endeavor to propagate are admitted for true, the consequences which, I think, evidently flow from thence are that atheism and skepticism will be utterly destroyed, many intricate points made plain, great difficulties solved, several useless parts of science retrenched, speculation referred to practice, and men reduced from paradoxes to common sense.

And, although it may, perhaps, seem an uneasy reflection to some that, when they have taken a circuit through so many refined and unvulgar notions, they should at last come to think like other men, yet, methinks, this return to the simple dictates of nature, after having wandered through the wild mazes of philosophy, is not unpleasant. It is like coming home from a long voyage: a man reflects with pleasure on the many difficulties and perplexities he has passed through, sets his heart at ease, and enjoys himself with more satisfaction for the future.

As it was my intention to convince skeptics and infidels by

reason, so it has been my endeavor strictly to observe the most
rigid laws of reasoning. And to an impartial reader I hope it
will be manifest that the sublime notion of a God and the
comfortable expectation of immortality do naturally arise from
a close and methodical application of thought—whatever may
be the result of that loose, rambling way, not altogether improperly termed Free-thinking, by certain libertines in thought
who can no more endure the restraints of logic than those of
religion or government.

It will, perhaps, be objected to my design that, so far as it
tends to ease the mind of difficult and useless inquiries, it can
affect only a few speculative persons; but if, by their speculations rightly placed, the study of morality and the law of nature
were brought more into fashion among men of parts and
genius, the discouragements that draw to skepticism removed,
the measures of right and wrong accurately defined, and the
principles of natural religion reduced into regular systems,
as artfully disposed and clearly connected as those of some
other sciences—there are grounds to think these effects would
not only have a gradual influence in repairing the too much
defaced sense of virtue in the world, but also, by showing that
such parts of revelation as lie within the reach of human inquiry are most agreeable to right reason, would dispose all
prudent, unprejudiced persons to a modest and wary treatment
of those sacred mysteries which are above the comprehension
of our faculties.

It remains that I desire the reader to withhold his censure
of these *Dialogues* till he has read them through. Otherwise he
may lay them aside, in a mistake of their design or on account
of difficulties or objections which he would find answered in
the sequel. A treatise of this nature would require to be once
read over coherently in order to comprehend its design, the
proofs, solution of difficulties, and the connection and disposi-
tion of its parts. If it be thought to deserve a second reading,
this, I imagine, will make the entire scheme very plain, especially if recourse be had to an essay I wrote some years since

upon *Vision,* and the *Treatise Concerning the Principles of Human Knowledge*—wherein divers notions advanced in these *Dialogues* are further pursued or placed in different lights, and other points handled which naturally tend to confirm and illustrate them.

THREE DIALOGUES

BETWEEN HYLAS AND PHILONOUS, IN OPPOSITION TO SKEPTICS AND ATHEISTS

THE FIRST DIALOGUE

Philonous. Good morrow, Hylas. I did not expect to find you abroad so early.

Hylas. It is indeed something unusual; but my thoughts were so taken up with a subject I was discoursing of last night that, finding I could not sleep, I resolved to rise and take a turn in the garden.

Phil. It happened well, to let you see what innocent and agreeable pleasures you lose every morning. Can there be a pleasanter time of the day or a more delightful season of the year? That purple sky, these wild but sweet notes of birds, the fragrant bloom upon the trees and flowers, the gentle influence of the rising sun—these and a thousand nameless beauties of nature inspire the soul with secret transports; its faculties, too, being at this time fresh and lively, are fit for those meditations which the solitude of a garden and tranquility of the morning naturally dispose us to. But I am afraid I interrupt your thoughts, for you seemed very intent on something.

Hyl. It is true, I was, and shall be obliged to you if you will permit me to go on in the same vein; not that I would by any means deprive myself of your company, for my thoughts always flow more easily in conversation with a friend than when I am alone; but my request is that you would suffer me to impart my reflections to you.

Phil. With all my heart, it is what I should have requested myself if you had not prevented me.

Hyl. I was considering the odd fate of those men who have in all ages, through an affectation of being distinguished from

9

the vulgar, or some unaccountable turn of thought, pretended either to believe nothing at all or to believe the most extravagant things in the world. This, however, might be borne if their paradoxes and skepticism did not draw after them some consequences of general disadvantage to mankind. But the mischief lies here: that when men of less leisure see them who are supposed to have spent their whole time in the pursuits of knowledge professing an entire ignorance of all things or advancing such notions as are repugnant to plain and commonly received principles, they will be tempted to entertain suspicions concerning the most important truths, which they had hitherto held sacred and unquestionable.

Phil. I entirely agree with you as to the ill tendency of the affected doubts of some philosophers and fantastical conceits of others. I am even so far gone of late in this way of thinking that I have quitted several of the sublime notions I had got in their schools for vulgar opinions. And I give it you on my word, since this revolt from metaphysical notions to the plain dictates of nature and common sense, I find my understanding strangely enlightened, so that I can now easily comprehend a great many things which before were all mystery and riddle.

Hyl. I am glad to find there was nothing in the accounts I heard of you.

Phil. Pray, what were those?

Hyl. You were represented in last night's conversation as one who maintained the most extravagant opinion that ever entered into the mind of man, to wit, that there is no such thing as "material substance" in the world.

Phil. That there is no such thing as what philosophers call "material substance," I am seriously persuaded; but if I were made to see anything absurd or skeptical in this, I should then have the same reason to renounce this that I imagine I have now to reject the contrary opinion.

Hyl. What! Can anything be more fantastical, more repugnant to common sense or a more manifest piece of skepticism than to believe there is no such thing as matter?

Phil. Softly, good Hylas. What if it should prove that you, who hold there is, are, by virtue of that opinion, a greater skeptic and maintain more paradoxes and repugnances to common sense than I who believe no such thing?

Hyl. You may as soon persuade me the part is greater than the whole, as that, in order to avoid absurdity and skepticism, I should ever be obliged to give up my opinion in this point.

Phil. Well then, are you content to admit that opinion for true which, upon examination, shall appear most agreeable to common sense and remote from skepticism?

Hyl. With all my heart. Since you are for raising disputes about the plainest things in nature, I am content for once to hear what you have to say.

Phil. Pray, Hylas, what do you mean by a "skeptic?"

Hyl. I mean what all men mean, one that doubts of everything.

Phil. He then who entertains no doubt concerning some particular point, with regard to that point cannot be thought a skeptic.

Hyl. I agree with you.

Phil. Whether does doubting consist in embracing the affirmative or negative side of a question?

Hyl. In neither; for whoever understands English cannot but know that *doubting* signifies a suspense between both.

Phil. He then that denies any point can no more be said to doubt of it than he who affirms it with the same degree of assurance.

Hyl. True.

Phil. And, consequently, for such his denial is no more to be esteemed a skeptic than the other.

Hyl. I acknowledge it.

Phil. How comes it to pass then, Hylas, that you pronounce me a skeptic because I deny what you affirm, to wit, the existence of matter? Since, for aught you can tell, I am as peremptory in my denial as you in your affirmation.

Hyl. Hold, Philonous, I have been a little out in my definition; but every false step a man makes in discourse is not to be insisted on. I said indeed that a "skeptic" was one who doubted of everything; but I should have added: or who denies the reality and truth of things.

Phil. What things? Do you mean the principles and theorems of sciences? But these you know are universal intellectual notions, and consequently independent of matter; the denial therefore of this does not imply the denying them.

Hyl. I grant it. But are there no other things? What think you of distrusting the senses, of denying the real existence of sensible things, or pretending to know nothing of them. Is not this sufficient to denominate a man a skeptic?

Phil. Shall we therefore examine which of us it is that denies the reality of sensible things or professes the greatest ignorance of them, since, if I take you rightly, he is to be esteemed the greatest skeptic?

Hyl. That is what I desire.

* * *

Phil. What mean you by "sensible things?"

Hyl. Those things which are perceived by the senses. Can you imagine that I mean anything else?

Phil. Pardon me, Hylas, if I am desirous clearly to apprehend your notions, since this may much shorten our inquiry. Suffer me then to ask you this further question. Are those things only perceived by the senses which are perceived immediately? Or may those things properly be said to be "sensible" which are perceived mediately, or not without the intervention of others?

Hyl. I do not sufficiently understand you.

Phil. In reading a book, what I immediately perceive are the letters, but mediately, or by means of these, are suggested to my mind the notions of God, virtue, truth, etc. Now, that the letters are truly sensible things, or perceived by sense, there is no doubt; but I would know whether you take the things suggested by them to be so too.

Hyl. No, certainly; it were absurd to think God or virtue sensible things, though they may be signified and suggested to the mind by sensible marks with which they have an arbitrary connection.

Phil. It seems, then, that by "sensible things" you mean those only which can be perceived immediately by sense.

Hyl. Right.

Phil. Does it not follow from this that, though I see one part of the sky red, and another blue, and that my reason does thence evidently conclude there must be some cause of that diversity of colors, yet that cause cannot be said to be a sensible thing or perceived by the sense of seeing?

Hyl. It does.

Phil. In like manner, though I hear variety of sounds, yet I cannot be said to hear the causes of those sounds.

Hyl. You cannot.

Phil. And when by my touch I perceive a thing to be hot and heavy, I cannot say, with any truth or propriety, that I feel the cause of its heat or weight.

Hyl. To prevent any more questions of this kind, I tell you once for all that by "sensible things" I mean those only which are perceived by sense, and that in truth the senses perceive nothing which they do not perceive immediately, for they make no inferences. The deducing therefore of causes or occasions from effects and appearances, which alone are perceived by sense, entirely relates to reason.

Phil. This point then is agreed between us—that *sensible things are those only which are immediately perceived by sense.* You will further inform me whether we immediately perceive by sight anything besides light and colors and figures; or by hearing, anything but sounds; by the palate, anything beside tastes; by the smell, besides odors; or by the touch, more than tangible qualities.

Hyl. We do not.

Phil. It seems, therefore, that if you take away all sensible qualities, there remains nothing sensible?

Hyl. I grant it.

Phil. Sensible things therefore are nothing else but so many sensible qualities or combinations of sensible qualities?

Hyl. Nothing else.

Phil. Heat is then a sensible thing?

Hyl. Certainly.

Phil. Does the reality of sensible things consist in being perceived, or is it something distinct from their being perceived, and that bears no relation to the mind?

Hyl. To *exist* is one thing, and to be *perceived* is another.

Phil. I speak with regard to sensible things only; and of these I ask, whether by their real existence you mean a subsistence exterior to the mind and distinct from their being perceived?

Hyl. I mean a real absolute being, distinct from and without any relation to their being perceived.

Phil. Heat therefore, if it be allowed a real being, must exist without the mind?

Hyl. It must.

Phil. Tell me, Hylas, is this real existence equally compatible to all degrees of heat, which we perceive, or is there any reason why we should attribute it to some and deny it to others? And if there be, pray let me know that reason.

Hyl. Whatever degree of heat we perceive by sense, we may be sure the same exists in the object that occasions it.

Phil. What! the greatest as well as the least?

Hyl. I tell you, the reason is plainly the same in respect of both: they are both perceived by sense; nay, the greater degree of heat is more sensibly perceived; and consequently, if there is any difference, we are more certain of its real existence than we can be of the reality of a lesser degree.

Phil. But is not the most vehement and intense degree of heat a very great pain?

Hyl. No one can deny it.

Phil. And is any unperceiving thing capable of pain or pleasure?

Hyl. No, certainly.

Phil. Is your material substance a senseless being or a being endowed with sense and perception?

Hyl. It is senseless, without doubt.

Phil. It cannot, therefore, be the subject of pain?

Hyl. By no means.

Phil. Nor, consequently, of the greatest heat perceived by sense, since you acknowledge this to be no small pain?

Hyl. I grant it.

Phil. What shall we say then of your external object: is it a material substance, or no?

Hyl. It is a material substance with the sensible qualities inhering in it.

Phil. How then can a great heat exist in it, since you own it cannot in a material substance? I desire you would clear this point.

Hyl. Hold, Philonous, I fear I was out in yielding intense heat to be a pain. It should seem rather that pain is something distinct from heat, and the consequence or effect of it.

Phil. Upon putting your hand near the fire, do you perceive one simple uniform sensation or two distinct sensations?

Hyl. But one simple sensation.

Phil. Is not the heat immediately perceived?

Hyl. It is.

Phil. And the pain?

Hyl. True.

Phil. Seeing therefore they are both immediately perceived at the same time, and the fire affects you only with one simple or uncompounded idea, it follows that this same simple idea is both the intense heat immediately perceived and the pain; and, consequently, that the intense heat immediately perceived is nothing distinct from a particular sort of pain.

Hyl. It seems so.

Phil. Again, try in your thoughts, Hylas, if you can conceive a vehement sensation to be without pain or pleasure.

Hyl. I cannot.

Phil. Or can you frame to yourself an idea of sensible pain or pleasure, in general, abstracted from every particular idea of heat, cold, tastes, smells, etc.?

Hyl. I do not find that I can.

Phil. Does it not therefore follow that sensible pain is nothing distinct from those sensations or ideas—in an intense degree?

Hyl. It is undeniable; and, to speak the truth, I begin to suspect a very great heat cannot exist but in a mind perceiving it.

Phil. What! are you then in that *skeptical* state of suspense, between affirming and denying?

Hyl. I think I may be positive in the point. A very violent and painful heat cannot exist without the mind.

Phil. It has not therefore, according to you, any real being?

Hyl. I own it.

Phil. Is it therefore certain that there is no body in nature really hot?

Hyl. I have not denied there is any real heat in bodies. I only say there is no such thing as an intense real heat.

Phil. But did you not say before that all degrees of heat were equally real, or, if there was any difference, that the greater were more undoubtedly real than the lesser?

Hyl. True; but it was because I did not then consider the ground there is for distinguishing between them, which I now plainly see. And it is this: because intense heat is nothing else but a particular kind of painful sensation, and pain cannot exist but in a perceiving being, it follows that no intense heat can really exist in an unperceiving corporeal substance. But this is no reason why we should deny heat in an inferior degree to exist in such a substance.

Phil. But how shall we be able to discern those degrees of heat which exist only in the mind from those which exist without it?

Hyl. That is no difficult matter. You know the least pain cannot exist unperceived; whatever, therefore, degree of heat is a pain exists only in the mind. But as for all other degrees of heat nothing obliges us to think the same of them.

Phil. I think you granted before that no unperceiving being was capable of pleasure any more than of pain.

Hyl. I did.

Phil. And is not warmth, or a more gentle degree of heat than what causes uneasiness, a pleasure?

Hyl. What then?

Phil. Consequently, it cannot exist without the mind in an unperceiving substance, or body.

Hyl. So it seems.

Phil. Since, therefore, as well those degrees of heat that are not painful, as those that are, can exist only in a thinking substance, may we not conclude that external bodies are absolutely incapable of any degree of heat whatsoever?

Hyl. On second thoughts, I do not think it is so evident that warmth is a pleasure as that a great degree of heat is a pain.

Phil. I do not pretend that warmth is as great a pleasure as heat is a pain. But if you grant it to be even a small pleasure, it serves to make good my conclusion.

Hyl. I could rather call it an "indolence." It seems to be nothing more than a privation of both pain and pleasure. And that such a quality or state as this may agree to an unthinking substance, I hope you will not deny.

Phil. If you are resolved to maintain that warmth, or a gentle degree of heat, is no pleasure, I know not how to convince you otherwise than by appealing to your own sense. But what think you of cold?

Hyl. The same that I do of heat. An intense degree of cold is a pain; for to feel a very great cold is to perceive a great uneasiness; it cannot therefore exist without the mind; but a lesser degree of cold may, as well as a lesser degree of heat.

Phil. Those bodies, therefore, upon whose application to our own we perceive a moderate degree of heat must be concluded to have a moderate degree of heat or warmth in them; and those upon whose application we feel a like degree of cold must be thought to have cold in them.

Hyl. They must.

Phil. Can any doctrine be true that necessarily leads a man into an absurdity?

Hyl. Without doubt it cannot.

Phil. Is it not an absurdity to think that the same thing should be at the same time both cold and warm?

Hyl. It is.

Phil. Suppose now one of your hands hot, and the other cold, and that they are both at once put into the same vessel of water, in an intermediate state, will not the water seem cold to one hand, and warm to the other?

Hyl. It will.

Phil. Ought we not therefore, by your principles, to conclude it is really both cold and warm at the same time, that is, according to your own concession, to believe an absurdity?

Hyl. I confess it seems so.

Phil. Consequently, the principles themselves are false, since you have granted that no true principle leads to an absurdity.

Hyl. But, after all, can anything be more absurd than to say, *there is no heat in the fire?*

Phil. To make the point still clearer; tell me whether, in two cases exactly alike, we ought not to make the same judgment?

Hyl. We ought.

Phil. When a pin pricks your finger, does it not rend and divide the fibres of your flesh?

Hyl. It does.

Phil. And when a coal burns your finger, does it any more?

Hyl. It does not.

Phil. Since, therefore, you neither judge the sensation itself occasioned by the pin, nor anything like it to be in the pin, you should not, conformably to what you have now granted, judge the sensation occasioned by the fire, or anything like it, to be in the fire.

Hyl. Well, since it must be so, I am content to yield this point and acknowledge that heat and cold are only sensations existing in our minds. But there still remain qualities enough to secure the reality of external things.

Phil. But what will you say, Hylas, if it shall appear that the case is the same with regard to all other sensible qualities,

[handwritten margin note: There is no heat without the mind, but also no fire without the mind.]

[handwritten margin note: But are they exactly alike?]

and that they can no more be supposed to exist without the mind than heat and cold?

Hyl. Then, indeed, you will have done something to the purpose; but that is what I despair of seeing proved.

Phil. Let us examine them in order. What think you of tastes—do they exist without the mind, or no?

Hyl. Can any man in his senses doubt whether sugar is sweet, or wormwood bitter?

Phil. Inform me, Hylas. Is a sweet taste a particular kind of pleasure or pleasant sensation, or is it not?

Hyl. It is.

Phil. And is not bitterness some kind of uneasiness or pain?

Hyl. I grant it.

Phil. If, therefore, sugar and wormwood are unthinking corporeal substances existing without the mind, how can sweetness and bitterness, that is, pleasure and pain, agree to them?

Hyl. Hold, Philonous. I now see what it was [that] deluded me all this time. You asked whether heat and cold, sweetness and bitterness, were not particular sorts of pleasure and pain; to which I answered simply that they were. Whereas I should have thus distinguished: those qualities as perceived by us are pleasures or pains, but not as existing in the external objects. We must not therefore conclude absolutely that there is no heat in the fire or sweetness in the sugar, but only that heat or sweetness, as perceived by us, are not in the fire or sugar. What say you to this?

Phil. I say it is nothing to the purpose. Our discourse proceeded altogether concerning sensible things, which you defined to be "the things we immediately perceive by our senses." Whatever other qualities, therefore, you speak of, as distinct from these, I know nothing of them, neither do they at all belong to the point in dispute. You may, indeed, pretend to have discovered certain qualities which you do not perceive and assert those insensible qualities exist in fire and sugar. But what use can be made of this to your present purpose, I am at a loss to conceive. Tell me then once more, do you acknowledge that heat and cold, sweetness and bitterness (meaning those qualities which are perceived by the senses), do not exist without the mind?

Hyl. I see it is to no purpose to hold out, so I give up the cause as to those mentioned qualities, though I profess it sounds oddly to say that sugar is not sweet.

Phil. But, for your further satisfaction, take this along with you: that which at other times seems sweet shall, to a distempered palate, appear bitter. And nothing can be plainer than that divers persons perceive different tastes in the same food, since that which one man delights in, another abhors. And how could this be if the taste was something really inherent in the food?

relativity factor

Hyl. I acknowledge I know not how.

Phil. In the next place, odors are to be considered. And with regard to these I would fain know whether what has been said of tastes does not exactly agree to them? Are they not so many pleasing or displeasing sensations?

Hyl. They are.

Phil. Can you then conceive it possible that they should exist in an unperceiving thing?

Hyl. I cannot.

Phil. Or can you imagine that filth and ordure affect those brute animals that feed on them out of choice with the same smells which we perceive in them?

Hyl. By no means.

Phil. May we not therefore conclude of smells, as of the other forementioned qualities, that they cannot exist in any but a perceiving substance or mind?

Hyl. I think so.

similar to page 14

Phil. Then as to sounds, what must we think of them, are they accidents really inherent in external bodies or not?

Hyl. That they inhere not in the sonorous bodies is plain from hence; because a bell struck in the exhausted receiver of an air-pump sends forth no sound. The air, therefore, must be thought the subject of sound.

Phil. What reason is there for that, Hylas?

Hyl. Because, when any motion is raised in the air, we perceive a sound greater or lesser, in proportion to the air's motion; but without some motion in the air we never hear any sound at all.

Phil. And granting that we never hear a sound but when some motion is produced in the air, yet I do not see how you can infer from thence that the sound itself is in the air.

Hyl. It is this very motion in the external air that produces in the mind the sensation of sound. For, striking on the drum of the ear, it causes a vibration which by the auditory nerves being communicated to the brain, the soul is thereupon affected with the sensation called "sound."

Phil. What! is sound then a sensation?

Hyl. I tell you, as perceived by us it is a particular sensation in the mind.

Phil. And can any sensation exist without the mind?

Hyl. No, certainly.

Phil. How then can sound, being a sensation, exist in the air if by the "air" you mean a senseless substance existing without the mind?

Hyl. You must distinguish, Philonous, between sound as it is perceived by us, and as it is in itself; or (which is the same thing) between the sound we immediately perceive and that which exists without us. The former, indeed, is a particular kind of sensation, but the latter is merely a vibrative or undulatory motion in the air.

Phil. I thought I had already obviated that distinction by the answer I gave when you were applying it in a like case before. But, to say no more of that, are you sure then that sound is really nothing but motion?

Hyl. I am.

Phil. Whatever, therefore, agrees to real sound may with truth be attributed to motion?

Hyl. It may.

Phil. It is then good sense to speak of "motion" as of a thing that is *loud, sweet, acute,* or *grave.*

Hyl. I see you are resolved not to understand me. Is it not evident those accidents or modes belong only to sensible sound, or sound in the common acceptation of the word, but not to sound in the real and philosophic sense, which, as I just now told you, is nothing but a certain motion of the air?

Phil. It seems then there are two sorts of sound—the one vulgar, or that which is heard, the other philosophical and real?

Hyl. Even so.

Phil. And the latter consists in motion?

Hyl. I told you so before.

Phil. Tell me, Hylas, to which of the senses, think you, the idea of motion belongs? To the hearing?

Hyl. No, certainly; but to the sight and touch.

Phil. It should follow then that, according to you, real sounds may possibly be *seen* or *felt,* but never *heard.*

Hyl. Look you, Philonous, you may, if you please, make a jest of my opinion, but that will not alter the truth of things. I own, indeed, the inferences you draw me into sound something oddly, but common language, you know, is framed by, and for the use of, the vulgar. We must not therefore wonder if expressions adapted to exact philosophic notions seem uncouth and out of the way.

Phil. Is it come to that? I assure you I imagine myself to have gained no small point since you make so light of departing from common phrases and opinions, it being a main part of our inquiry to examine whose notions are widest of the common road and most repugnant to the general sense of the world. But can you think it no more than a philosophical paradox to say that "real sounds are never heard," and that the idea of them is obtained by some other sense? And is there nothing in this contrary to nature and the truth of things?

Hyl. To deal ingenuously, I do not like it. And, after the concessions already made, I had as well grant that sounds, too, have no real being without the mind.

Phil. And I hope you will make no difficulty to acknowledge the same of colors.

Hyl. Pardon me; the case of colors is very different. Can anything be plainer than that we see them on the objects?

Phil. The objects you speak of are, I suppose, corporeal substances existing without the mind?

Hyl. They are.

Phil. And have true and real colors inhering in them?

Hyl. Each visible object has that color which we see in it.

Phil. How! is there anything visible but what we perceive by sight?

Hyl. There is not.

Phil. And do we perceive anything by sense which we do not perceive immediately?

Hyl. How often must I be obliged to repeat the same thing? I tell you, we do not.

Phil. Have patience, good Hylas, and tell me once more whether there is anything immediately perceived by the senses except sensible qualities. I know you asserted there was not; but I would now be informed whether you still persist in the same opinion.

Hyl. I do.

Phil. Pray, is your corporeal substance either a sensible quality or made up of sensible qualities?

Hyl. What a question that is! Who ever thought it was?

Phil. My reason for asking was, because in saying "each visible object has that color which we see in it," you make visible objects to be corporeal substances, which implies either that corporeal substances are sensible qualities or else that there is something besides sensible qualities perceived by sight; but as this point was formerly agreed between us, and is still maintained by you, it is a clear consequence that your corporeal substance is nothing distinct from sensible qualities.

Hyl. You may draw as many absurd consequences as you please and endeavor to perplex the plainest things, but you shall never persuade me out of my senses. I clearly understand my own meaning.

Phil. I wish you would make me understand it, too. But,

since you are unwilling to have your notion of corporeal substance examined, I shall urge that point no further. Only be pleased to let me know whether the same colors which we see exist in external bodies or some other.

Hyl. The very same.

Phil. What! are then the beautiful red and purple we see on yonder clouds really in them? Or do you imagine they have in themselves any other form than that of a dark mist or vapor?

Hyl. I must own, Philonous, those colors are not really in the clouds as they seem to be at this distance. They are only apparent colors.

Phil. "Apparent" call you them? How shall we distinguish these apparent colors from real?

Hyl. Very easily. Those are to be thought apparent which, appearing only at a distance, vanish upon a nearer approach.

Phil. And those, I suppose, are to be thought real which are discovered by the most near and exact survey.

Hyl. Right.

Phil. Is the nearest and exactest survey made by the help of a microscope or by the naked eye?

Hyl. By a microscope, doubtless.

Phil. But a microscope often discovers colors in an object different from those perceived by the unassisted sight. And, in case we had microscopes magnifying to any assigned degree, it is certain that no object whatsoever, viewed through them, would appear in the same color which it exhibits to the naked eye.

Hyl. And what will you conclude from all this? You cannot argue that there are really and naturally no colors on objects because by artificial managements they may be altered or made to vanish.

Phil. I think it may evidently be concluded from your own concessions that all the colors we see with our naked eyes are only apparent as those on the clouds, since they vanish upon a more close and accurate inspection which is afforded us by a microscope. Then, as to what you say by way of prevention: I ask you whether the real and natural state of an object is better discovered by a very sharp and piercing sight or by one which is less sharp?

Hyl. By the former without doubt.

Phil. Is it not plain from dioptrics that microscopes make the sight more penetrating and represent objects as they would appear to the eye in case it were naturally endowed with a most exquisite sharpness?

Hyl. It is.

Phil. Consequently, the microscopical representation is to be thought that which best sets forth the real nature of the thing, or what it is in itself. The colors, therefore, by it perceived are more genuine and real than those perceived otherwise.

Hyl. I confess there is something in what you say.

Phil. Besides, it is not only possible but manifest that there actually are animals whose eyes are by nature framed to perceive those things which by reason of their minuteness escape our sight. What think you of those inconceivably small animals perceived by glasses? Must we suppose they are all stark blind? Or, in case they see, can it be imagined their sight has not the same use in preserving their bodies from injuries which appears in that of all other animals? And if it has, is it not evident they must see particles less than their own bodies, which will present them with a far different view in each object from that which strikes our senses? Even our own eyes do not always represent objects to us after the same manner. In the jaundice everyone knows that all things seem yellow. Is it not therefore highly probable those animals in whose eyes we discern a very different texture from that of ours, and whose bodies abound with different humors, do not see the same colors in every object that we do? From all which should it not seem to follow that all colors are equally apparent, and that none of those which we perceive are really inherent in any outward object?

Hyl. It should.

Phil. The point will be past all doubt if you consider that, in case colors were real properties or affections inherent in external bodies, they could admit of no alteration without some change wrought in the very bodies themselves; but is it not evident from what has been said that, upon the use of microscopes, upon a change happening in the humors of the eye, or a variation of distance, without any manner of real alteration in the thing itself, the colors of any object are either changed or totally disappear? Nay, all other circumstances remaining the same, change but the situation of some objects and they shall present different colors to the eye. The same thing happens upon viewing an object in various degrees of light. And what is more known than that the same bodies appear differently colored by candlelight from what they do in the open day? Add to these the experiment of a prism which, separating the heterogeneous rays of light, alters the color of any object and will cause the whitest to appear of a deep blue or red to the naked eye. And now tell me whether you are still of opinion that every body has its true real color inhering in it; and if you think it has, I would fain know further from you what certain distance and position of the object, what peculiar texture and formation of the eye, what degree or kind of light is necessary for ascertaining that true color and distinguishing it from apparent ones.

Hyl. I own myself entirely satisfied that they are all equally apparent and that there is no such thing as color really inhering in external bodies, but that it is altogether in the light. And what confirms me in this opinion is that in proportion to the light colors are still more or less vivid; and if there be no light, then are there no colors perceived. Besides, allowing there are colors on external objects, yet, how is it possible for us to perceive them? For no external body affects the mind unless it acts first on our organs of sense. But the only action of bodies is motion, and motion cannot be communicated otherwise than by impulse. A distant object, therefore, cannot act on the eye, nor consequently make itself or its properties perceivable to the soul. Whence it plainly follows that it is immediately some contiguous substance which, operating on the eye, occasions a perception of colors; and such is light.

Phil. How! is light then a substance?

Hyl. I tell you, Philonous, external light is nothing but a thin fluid substance whose minute particles, being agitated with a brisk motion and in various manners reflected from the different surfaces of outward objects to the eyes, communicate different motions to the optic nerves; which, being propagated to the brain, cause therein various impressions, and these are attended with the sensations of red, blue, yellow, etc.

Phil. It seems, then, the light does no more than shake the optic nerves.

Hyl. Nothing else.

Phil. And, consequent to each particular motion of the nerves, the mind is affected with a sensation which is some particular color.

Hyl. Right.

Phil. And these sensations have no existence without the mind.

Hyl. They have not.

Phil. How then do you affirm that colors are in the light, since by "light" you understand a corporeal substance external to the mind?

Hyl. Light and colors, as immediately perceived by us, I grant cannot exist without the mind. But in themselves they are only the motions and configurations of certain insensible particles of matter.

Phil. Colors, then, in the vulgar sense, or taken for the immediate objects of sight, cannot agree to any but a perceiving substance.

Hyl. That is what I say.

Phil. Well then, since you give up the point as to those sensible qualities which are alone thought colors by all mankind besides, you may hold what you please with regard to those invisible ones of the philosophers. It is not my business to dispute about them; only I would advise you to bethink yourself whether, considering the inquiry we are upon, it be prudent for you to affirm—*the red and blue which we see are not real colors, but certain unknown motions and figures which no man ever did or can see are truly so.* Are not these shocking notions, and are not they subject to as many ridiculous inferences as those you were obliged to renounce before in the case of sounds?

Hyl. I frankly own, Philonous, that it is in vain to stand out any longer. Colors, sounds, tastes, in a word, all those termed "secondary qualities," have certainly no existence without the mind. But by this acknowledgment I must not be supposed to derogate anything from the reality of matter or external objects; seeing it is no more than several philosophers maintain, who nevertheless are the farthest imaginable from denying matter. For the clearer understanding of this you must know sensible qualities are by philosophers divided into "primary" and "secondary." The former are extension, figure, solidity, gravity, motion, and rest. And these they hold exist really in bodies. The latter are those above enumerated, or, briefly, all sensible qualities besides the primary, which they assert are only so many sensations or ideas existing nowhere but in the mind. But all this, I doubt not, you are already apprised of. For my part I have been a long time sensible there was such an opinion current among philosophers, but was never thoroughly convinced of its truth till now.

Phil. You are still then of opinion that *extension* and *figures* are inherent in external unthinking substances?

Hyl. I am.

Phil. But what if the same arguments which are brought against secondary qualities will hold good against these also?

Hyl. Why then I shall be obliged to think they too exist only in the mind.

Phil. Is it your opinion the very figure and extension which you perceive by sense exist in the outward object or material substance?

Hyl. It is.

Phil. Have all other animals as good grounds to think the same of the figure and extension which they see and feel?

Hyl. Without doubt, if they have any thought at all.

Phil. Answer me, Hylas. Think you the senses were bestowed upon all animals for their preservation and well-being in life? Or were they given to men alone for this end?

Hyl. I make no question but they have the same use in all other animals.

Phil. If so, is it not necessary they should be enabled by them to perceive their own limbs and those bodies which are capable of harming them?

Hyl. Certainly.

Phil. A mite therefore must be supposed to see his own foot, and things equal or even less than it, as bodies of some considerable dimension, though at the same time they appear to you scarce discernible or at best as so many visible points?

Hyl. I cannot deny it.

Phil. And to creatures less than the mite they will seem yet larger?

Hyl. They will.

Phil. Insomuch that what you can hardly discern will to another extremely minute animal appear as some huge mountain?

Hyl. All this I grant.

Phil. Can one and the same thing be at the same time in itself of different dimensions?

Hyl. That were absurd to imagine.

Phil. But from what you have laid down it follows that both the extension by you perceived and that perceived by the mite itself, as likewise all those perceived by lesser animals, are each of them the true extension of the mite's foot; that is to say, by your own principles you are led into an absurdity.

Hyl. There seems to be some difficulty in the point.

Phil. Again, have you not acknowledged that no real inherent property of any object can be changed without some change in the thing itself?

Hyl. I have.

Phil. But, as we approach to or recede from an object, the visible extension varies, being at one distance ten or a hundred times greater than at another. Does it not therefore follow from hence likewise that it is not really inherent in the object?

Hyl. I own I am at a loss what to think.

Phil. Your judgment will soon be determined if you will venture to think as freely concerning this quality as you have done concerning the rest. Was it not admitted as a good argument that neither heat nor cold was in the water because it seemed warm to one hand and cold to the other?

Hyl. It was.

Phil. Is it not the very same reasoning to conclude there is no extension or figure in an object because to one eye it shall seem little, smooth, and round, when at the same time it appears to the other great, uneven, and angular?

Hyl. The very same. But does this latter fact ever happen?

Phil. You may at any time make the experiment by looking with one eye bare, and with the other through a microscope.

Hyl. I know not how to maintain it, and yet I am loath to give up *extension;* I see so many odd consequences following upon such a concession.

Phil. Odd, say you? After the concessions already made, I hope you will stick at nothing for its oddness. [But,[1] on the other hand, should it not seem very odd if the general reasoning which includes all other sensible qualities did not also include extension? If it be allowed that no idea nor anything like an idea can exist in an unperceiving substance, then surely it follows that no figure or mode of extension, which we can either perceive or imagine, or have any idea of, can be really inherent in matter, not to mention the peculiar difficulty there must be in conceiving a material substance, prior to and distinct from extension, to be the *substratum* of extension. Be the sensible quality what it will—figure or sound or color—it seems alike impossible it should subsist in that which does not perceive it.]

Hyl. I give up the point for the present, reserving still a

[1] The remainder of the present paragraph did not appear in the first and second editions.

right to retract my opinion in case I shall hereafter discover any false step in my progress to it.

Phil. That is a right you cannot be denied. Figures and extension being dispatched, we proceed next to *motion.* Can a real motion in any external body be at the same time both very swift and very slow?

Hyl. It cannot.

Phil. Is not the motion of a body swift in a reciprocal proportion to the time it takes up in describing any given space? Thus a body that describes a mile in an hour moves three times faster than it would in case it described only a mile in three hours.

Hyl. I agree with you.

Phil. And is not time measured by the succession of ideas in our minds?

Hyl. It is.

Phil. And is it not possible ideas should succeed one another twice as fast in your mind as they do in mine, or in that of some spirit of another kind?

Hyl. I own it.

Phil. Consequently, the same body may to another seem to perform its motion over any space in half the time that it does to you. And the same reasoning will hold as to any other proportion; that is to say, according to your principles (since the motions perceived are both really in the object) it is possible one and the same body shall be really moved the same way at once, both very swift and very slow. How is this consistent either with common sense or with what you just now granted?

Hyl. I have nothing to say to it.

Phil. Then as for *solidity;* either you do not mean any sensible quality by that word, and so it is beside our inquiry; or if you do, it must be either hardness or resistance. But both the one and the other are plainly relative to our senses: it being evident that what seems hard to one animal may appear soft to another who has greater force and firmness of limbs.

But a person can't perceive an action before it takes place

What about solidity relative to some absolute standard?

Nor is it less plain that the resistance I feel is not in the body.

Hyl. I own the very sensation of resistance, which is all you immediately perceive, is not in the *body,* but the cause of that sensation is.

Phil. But the causes of our sensations are not things immediately perceived, and therefore not sensible. This point I thought had been already determined.

Hyl. I own it was; but you will pardon me if I seem a little embarrassed; I know not how to quit my old notions.

Phil. To help you out, do but consider that if *extension* be once acknowledged to have no existence without the mind, the same must necessarily be granted of motion, solidity, and gravity, since they all evidently suppose extension. It is therefore superfluous to inquire particularly concerning each of them. In denying extension, you have denied them all to have any real existence.

Hyl. I wonder, Philonous, if what you say be true, why those philosophers who deny the secondary qualities any real existence should yet attribute it to the primary. If there is no difference between them, how can this be accounted for?

Phil. It is not my business to account for every opinion of the philosophers. But, among other reasons which may be assigned for this, it seems probable that pleasure and pain being rather annexed to the former than the latter may be one. Heat and cold, tastes and smells have something more vividly pleasing or disagreeable than the ideas of extension, figure, and motion affect us with. And, it being too visibly absurd to hold that pain or pleasure can be in an unperceiving substance, men are more easily weaned from believing the external existence of the secondary than the primary qualities. You will be satisfied there is something in this if you recollect the difference you made between an intense and more moderate degree of heat, allowing the one a real existence while you denied it to the other. But, after all, there is no rational ground for that distinction, for surely an indifferent sensation is as truly a *sensation* as one more pleasing or painful, and consequently should not any more than they be supposed to exist in an unthinking subject.

Hyl. It is just come into my head, Philonous, that I have somewhere heard of a distinction between *absolute* and *sensible* extension. Now though it be acknowledged that *great* and *small,* consisting merely in the relation which other extended beings have to the parts of our own bodies, do not really inhere in the substances themselves, yet nothing obliges us to hold the same with regard to *absolute* extension, which is something abstracted from *great* and *small,* from this or that particular magnitude or figure. So likewise as to motion: *swift* and *slow* are altogether relative to the succession of ideas in our own minds. But it does not follow, because those modifications of motion exist not without the mind, that therefore absolute motion abstracted from them does not.

Phil. Pray what is it that distinguishes one motion, or one part of extension, from another? Is it not something sensible, as some degree of swiftness or slowness, some certain magnitude or figure peculiar to each?

Hyl. I think so.

Phil. These qualities, therefore, stripped of all sensible properties, are without all specific and numerical differences, as the schools call them.

Hyl. They are.

Phil. That is to say, they are extension in general, and motion in general.

Hyl. Let it be so.

Phil. But it is a universally received maxim that *everything which exists is particular.* How then can motion in general, or extension in general, exist in any corporeal substance?

Hyl. I will take time to solve your difficulty.

Phil. But I think the point may be speedily decided. Without doubt you can tell whether you are able to frame this or that idea. Now I am content to put our dispute on this issue. If you can frame in your thoughts a distinct abstract idea of motion or extension divested of all those sensible modes as

[margin, handwritten:] Representation of Abstract General Ideas

swift and slow, great and small, round and square, and the like, which are acknowledged to exist only in the mind, I will then yield the point you contend for. But if you cannot, it will be unreasonable on your side to insist any longer upon what you have no notion of.

Hyl. To confess ingenuously, I cannot.

Phil. Can you even separate the ideas of extension and motion from the ideas of all those qualities which they who make the distinction term "secondary?"

Hyl. What! is it not an easy matter to consider extension and motion by themselves, abstracted from all other sensible qualities? Pray how do the mathematicians treat of them?

Phil. I acknowledge, Hylas, it is not difficult to form general propositions and reasonings about those qualities without mentioning any other, and, in this sense, to consider or treat of them abstractedly. But how does it follow that, because I can pronounce the word "motion" by itself, I can form the idea of it in my mind exclusive of body? Or because theorems may be made of extension and figures, without any mention of *great* or *small,* or any other sensible mode or quality, that therefore it is possible such an abstract idea of extension, without any particular size or figure or sensible quality, should be distinctly formed and apprehended by the mind? Mathematicians treat of quantity without regarding what other sensible qualities it is attended with, as being altogether indifferent to their demonstrations. But when, laying aside the words, they contemplate the bare ideas, I believe you will find they are not the pure abstracted ideas of extension.

anti-Cartesian

Hyl. But what say you to *pure intellect?* May not abstracted ideas be framed by that faculty?

Phil. Since I cannot frame abstract ideas at all, it is plain I cannot frame them by the help of pure intellect, whatsoever faculty you understand by those words. Besides, not to inquire into the nature of pure intellect and its spiritual objects, as *virtue, reason, God,* or the like, thus much seems manifest that sensible things are only to be perceived by sense or represented by the imagination. Figures, therefore, and extension, being originally perceived by sense, do not belong to pure intellect; but, for your further satisfaction, try if you can frame the idea of any figure abstracted from all particularities of size or even from other sensible qualities.

Hyl. Let me think a little—— I do not find that I can.

Phil. And can you think it possible that should really exist in nature which implies a repugnancy in its conception?

Hyl. By no means.

Phil. Since therefore it is impossible even for the mind to disunite the ideas of extension and motion from all other sensible qualities, does it not follow that where the one exist there necessarily the other exist likewise?

Hyl. It should seem so.

Phil. Consequently, the very same arguments which you admitted as conclusive against the secondary qualities are, without any further application of force, against the primary, too. Besides, if you will trust your senses, is it not plain all sensible qualities coexist, or to them appear as being in the same place? Do they ever represent a motion or figure as being divested of all other visible and tangible qualities?

Hyl. You need say no more on this head. I am free to own, if there be no secret error or oversight in our proceedings hitherto, that all sensible qualities are alike to be denied existence without the mind. But my fear is that I have been too liberal in my former concessions, or overlooked some fallacy or other. In short, I did not take time to think.

Phil. For that matter, Hylas, you may take what time you please in reviewing the progress of our inquiry. You are at liberty to recover any slips you might have made, or offer whatever you have omitted which makes for your first opinion.

Hyl. One great oversight I take to be this—that I did not sufficiently distinguish the *object* from the *sensation*. Now, though this latter may not exist without the mind, yet it will not thence follow that the former cannot.

Phil. What object do you mean? The object of the senses?

Hyl. The same.

Phil. It is then immediately perceived?

Hyl. Right.

Phil. Make me to understand the difference between what is immediately perceived and a sensation.

Hyl. The sensation I take to be an act of the mind perceiving; besides which there is something perceived, and this I call the "object." For example, there is red and yellow on that tulip. But then the act of perceiving those colors is in me only, and not in the tulip.

Phil. What tulip do you speak of? Is it that which you see?

Hyl. The same.

Phil. And what do you see besides color, figure, and extension?

Hyl. Nothing.

Phil. What you would say then is that the red and yellow are coexistent with the extension; is it not?

Hyl. That is not all; I would say they have a real existence without the mind, in some unthinking substance.

Phil. That the colors are really in the tulip which I see is manifest. Neither can it be denied that this tulip may exist independent of your mind or mine; but that any immediate object of the senses—that is, any idea, or combination of ideas —should exist in an unthinking substance, or exterior to all minds, is in itself an evident contradiction. Nor can I imagine how this follows from what you said just now, to wit, that the red and yellow were on the tulip *you saw,* since you do not pretend to *see* that unthinking substance.

Hyl. You have an artful way, Philonous, of diverting our inquiry from the subject.

Phil. I see you have no mind to be pressed that way. To return then to your distinction between *sensation* and *object;* if I take you right, you distinguish in every perception two things, the one an action of the mind, the other not.

Hyl. True.

Phil. And this action cannot exist in, or belong to, any unthinking thing, but whatever besides is implied in a perception may?

Hyl. That is my meaning.

Phil. So that if there was a perception without any act of the mind, it were possible such a perception should exist in an unthinking substance?

Hyl. I grant it. But it is impossible there should be such a perception.

Phil. When is the mind said to be active?

Hyl. When it produces, puts an end to, or changes anything.

Phil. Can the mind produce, discontinue, or change anything but by an act of the will?

Hyl. It cannot.

Phil. The mind therefore is to be accounted *active* in its perceptions so far forth as *volition* is included in them?

Hyl. It is.

Phil. In plucking this flower I am active, because I do it by the motion of my hand, which was consequent upon my volition; so likewise in applying it to my nose. But is either of these smelling?

Hyl. No.

Phil. I act, too, in drawing the air through my nose, because my breathing so rather than otherwise is the effect of my volition. But neither can this be called "smelling," for if it were I should smell every time I breathed in that manner?

Hyl. True.

Phil. Smelling then is somewhat consequent to all this?

Hyl. It is.

Phil. But I do not find my will concerned any further. Whatever more there is—as that I perceive such a particular smell, or any smell at all—this is independent of my will, and therein I am altogether passive. Do you find it otherwise with you, Hylas?

Hyl. No, the very same.

Phil. Then, as to seeing, is it not in your power to open your eyes or keep them shut, to turn them this or that way?

Hyl. Without doubt.

Phil. But does it in like manner depend on your will that in looking on this flower you perceive *white* rather than any other color? Or, directing your open eyes toward yonder part of the heaven, can you avoid seeing the sun? Or is light or darkness the effect of your volition?

Hyl. No, certainly.

Phil. You are then in these respects altogether passive?

Hyl. I am.

Phil. Tell me now whether *seeing* consists in perceiving light and colors or in opening and turning the eyes?

Hyl. Without doubt, in the former.

Phil. Since, therefore, you are in the very perception of light and colors altogether passive, what is become of that action you were speaking of as an ingredient in every sensation? And does it not follow from your own concessions that the perception of light and colors, including no action in it, may exist in an unperceiving substance? And is not this a plain contradiction?

Hyl. I know not what to think of it.

Phil. Besides, since you distinguish the *active* and *passive* in every perception, you must do it in that of pain. But how is it possible that pain, be it as little active as you please, should exist in an unperceiving substance? In short, do but consider the point and then confess ingenuously whether light and colors, tastes, sounds, etc. are not all equally passions or sensations in the soul. You may indeed call them "external objects" and give them in words what subsistence you please. But examine your own thoughts and then tell me whether it be not as I say?

Hyl. I acknowledge, Philonous, that, upon a fair observation of what passes in my mind, I can discover nothing else but that I am a thinking being affected with variety of sensations, neither is it possible to conceive how a sensation should exist in an unperceiving substance. But then, on the other hand, when I look on sensible things in a different view, considering them as so many modes and qualities, I find it necessary to suppose a material *substratum,* without which they cannot be conceived to exist.

Phil. "Material substratum" call you it? Pray, by which of your senses came you acquainted with that being?

Hyl. It is not itself sensible; its modes and qualities only being perceived by the senses.

Phil. I presume then it was by reflection and reason you obtained the idea of it?

Hyl. I do not pretend to any proper positive idea of it. However, I conclude it exists because qualities cannot be conceived to exist without a support.

Phil. It seems then you have only a relative notion of it, or that you conceive it not otherwise than by conceiving the relation it bears to sensible qualities?

Hyl. Right.

Phil. Be pleased, therefore, to let me know wherein that relation consists.

Hyl. Is it not sufficiently expressed in the term "substratum" or "substance?"

Phil. If so, the word "substratum" should import that it is spread under the sensible qualities or accidents?

Hyl. True.

Phil. And consequently under extension?

Hyl. I own it.

Phil. It is therefore somewhat in its own nature entirely distinct from extension?

Hyl. I tell you extension is only a mode, and matter is something that supports modes. And is it not evident the thing supported is different from the thing supporting?

Phil. So that something distinct from, and exclusive of, extension is supposed to be the *substratum* of extension?

Hyl. Just so.

Phil. Answer me, Hylas, can a thing be spread without extension, or is not the idea of extension necessarily included in *spreading?*

Hyl. It is.

Phil. Whatsoever therefore you suppose spread under anything must have in itself an extension distinct from the extension of that thing under which it is spread?

Hyl. It must.

Phil. Consequently, every corporeal substance being the

substratum of extension must have in itself another extension by which it is qualified to be a *substratum,* and so on to infinity? And I ask whether this be not absurd in itself and repugnant to what you granted just now, to wit, that the *substratum* was something distinct from and exclusive of extension?

Hyl. Aye, but, Philonous, you take me wrong. I do not mean that matter is *spread* in a gross literal sense under extension. The word "substratum" is used only to express in general the same thing with "substance."

Phil. Well then, let us examine the relation implied in the term "substance." Is it not that it stands under accidents?

Hyl. The very same.

Phil. But that one thing may stand under or support another, must it not be extended?

Hyl. It must.

Phil. Is not therefore this supposition liable to the same absurdity with the former?

Hyl. You still take things in a strict literal sense; that is not fair, Philonous.

Phil. I am not for imposing any sense on your words; you are at liberty to explain them as you please. Only, I beseech you, make me understand something by them. You tell me matter supports or stands under accidents. How! is it as your legs support your body?

Hyl. No; that is the literal sense.

Phil. Pray let me know any sense, literal or not literal, that you understand it in.—— How long must I wait for an answer, Hylas?

Hyl. I declare I know not what to say. I once thought I understood well enough what was meant by matter's supporting accidents. But now, the more I think on it, the less can I comprehend it; in short, I find that I know nothing of it.

Phil. It seems then you have no idea at all, neither relative nor positive, of matter; you know neither what it is in itself nor what relation it bears to accidents?

Hyl. I acknowledge it.

Phil. And yet you asserted that you could not conceive how qualities or accidents should really exist without conceiving at the same time a material support of them?

Hyl. I did.

Phil. That is to say, when you conceive the real existence of qualities, you do withal conceive something which you cannot conceive?

Hyl. It was wrong I own. But still I fear there is some fallacy or other. Pray, what think you of this? It is just come into my head that the ground of all our mistake lies in your treating of each quality by itself. Now I grant that each quality cannot singly subsist without the mind. Color cannot without extension, neither can figure without some other sensible quality. But, as the several qualities united or blended together form entire sensible things, nothing hinders why such things may not be supposed to exist without the mind.

Phil. Either, Hylas, you are jesting or have a very bad memory. Though, indeed, we went through all the qualities by name one after another, yet my arguments, or rather your concessions, nowhere tended to prove that the secondary qualities did not subsist each alone by itself, but that they were not *at all* without the mind. Indeed, in treating of figure and motion we concluded they could not exist without the mind, because it was impossible even in thought to separate them from all secondary qualities, so as to conceive them existing by themselves. But then this was not the only argument made use of upon that occasion. But (to pass by all that has been hitherto said and reckon it for nothing, if you will have it so) I am content to put the whole upon this issue. If you can conceive it possible for any mixture or combination of qualities, or any sensible object whatever, to exist without the mind, then I will grant it actually to be so.

Hyl. If it comes to that the point will soon be decided. What more easy than to conceive a tree or house existing by itself, independent of, and unperceived by, any mind whatsoever? I do at this present time conceive them existing after that manner.

Phil. How say you, Hylas, can you see a thing which is at the same time unseen?

Hyl. No, that were a contradiction.

Phil. Is it not as great a contradiction to talk of *conceiving* a thing which is *unconceived?*

Hyl. It is.

Phil. The tree or house, therefore, which you think of is conceived by you?

Hyl. How should it be otherwise?

Phil. And what is conceived is surely in the mind?

Hyl. Without question, that which is conceived is in the mind.

Phil. How then came you to say you conceived a house or tree existing independent and out of all minds whatsoever?

Hyl. That was I own an oversight, but stay, let me consider what led me into it.—It is a pleasant mistake enough. As I was thinking of a tree in a solitary place where no one was present to see it, methought that was to conceive a tree as existing unperceived or unthought of, not considering that I myself conceived it all the while. But now I plainly see that all I can do is to frame ideas in my own mind. I may indeed conceive in my own thoughts the idea of a tree, or a house, or a mountain, but that is all. And this is far from proving that I can conceive them *existing out of the minds of all spirits.*

Phil. You acknowledge then that you cannot possibly conceive how any one corporeal sensible thing should exist otherwise than in a mind?

Hyl. I do.

Phil. And yet you will earnestly contend for the truth of that which you cannot so much as conceive?

Hyl. I profess I know not what to think; but still there are some scruples remain with me. Is it not certain I see things at a distance? Do we not perceive the stars and moon, for example, to be a great way off? Is not this, I say, manifest to the senses?

Phil. Do you not in a dream, too, perceive those or the like objects?

Hyl. I do.

Phil. And have they not then the same appearance of being distant?

Hyl. They have.

Phil. But you do not thence conclude the apparitions in a dream to be without the mind?

Hyl. By no means.

Phil. You ought not therefore to conclude that sensible objects are without the mind, from their appearance or manner wherein they are perceived.

Hyl. I acknowledge it. But does not my sense deceive me in those cases?

Phil. By no means. The idea or thing which you immediately perceive, neither sense nor reason informs you that it actually exists without the mind. By sense you only know that you are affected with such certain sensations of light and colors, etc. And these you will not say are without the mind.

Hyl. True, but, besides all that, do you not think the sight suggests something of *outness* or *distance?*

Phil. Upon approaching a distant object, do the visible size and figure change perpetually or do they appear the same at all distances?

Hyl. They are in a continual change.

Phil. Sight, therefore, does not suggest or any way inform you that the visible object you immediately perceive exists at a distance,[2] or will be perceived when you advance farther onward, there being a continued series of visible objects succeeding each other during the whole time of your approach.

Hyl. It does not; but still I know, upon seeing an object, what object I shall perceive after having passed over a certain distance; no matter whether it be exactly the same or no, there is still something of distance suggested in the case.

Phil. Good Hylas, do but reflect a little on the point, and then tell me whether there be any more in it than this. From the ideas you actually perceive by sight, you have by experience

[2] See the author's *An Essay towards a New Theory of Vision* (1709) and *The Theory of Vision Vindicated and Explained* (1733).

learned to collect what other ideas you will (according to the standing order of nature) be affected with, after such a certain succession of time and motion.

Hyl. Upon the whole, I take it to be nothing else.

Phil. Now is it not plain that if we suppose a man born blind was on a sudden made to see, he could at first have no experience of what may be suggested by sight?

Hyl. It is.

Phil. He would not then, according to you, have any notion of distance annexed to the things he saw, but would take them for a new set of sensations existing only in his mind?

Hyl. It is undeniable.

Phil. But to make it still more plain: is not *distance* a line turned endwise to the eye?

Hyl. It is.

Phil. And can a line so situated be perceived by sight?

Hyl. It cannot.

Phil. Does it not therefore follow that distance is not properly and immediately perceived by sight?

Hyl. It should seem so.

Phil. Again, it is your opinion that colors are at a distance?

Hyl. It must be acknowledged they are only in the mind.

Phil. But do not colors appear to the eye as coexisting in the same place with extension and figures?

Hyl. They do.

Phil. How can you then conclude from sight that figures exist without, when you acknowledge colors do not; the sensible appearance being the very same with regard to both?

Hyl. I know not what to answer.

Phil. But allowing that distance was truly and immediately perceived by the mind, yet it would not thence follow it existed out of the mind. For whatever is immediately perceived is an idea; and can any *idea* exist out of the mind?

Hyl. To suppose that were absurd; but, inform me, Philonous, can we perceive or know nothing besides our ideas?

Phil. As for the rational deducing of causes from effects, that is beside our inquiry. And by the senses you can best tell whether you perceive anything which is not immediately perceived. And I ask you whether the things immediately perceived are other than your own sensations or ideas? You have indeed more than once, in the course of this conversation, declared yourself on those points, but you seem, by this last question, to have departed from what you then thought.

Hyl. To speak the truth, Philonous, I think there are two kinds of objects: the one perceived immediately, which are likewise called "ideas"; the other are real things or external objects, perceived by the mediation of ideas which are their images and representations. Now I own ideas do not exist without the mind, but the latter sort of objects do. I am sorry I did not think of this distinction sooner; it would probably have cut short your discourse.

Phil. Are those external objects perceived by sense or by some other faculty?

Hyl. They are perceived by sense.

Phil. How! is there anything perceived by sense which is not immediately perceived?

Hyl. Yes, Philonous, in some sort there is. For example, when I look on a picture or statue of Julius Caesar, I may be said, after a manner, to perceive him (though not immediately) by my senses.

Phil. It seems then you will have our ideas, which alone are immediately perceived, to be pictures of external things: and that these also are perceived by sense inasmuch as they have a conformity or resemblance to our ideas?

Hyl. That is my meaning.

Phil. And in the same way that Julius Caesar, in himself invisible, is nevertheless perceived by sight, real things, in themselves imperceptible, are perceived by sense.

Hyl. In the very same.

Phil. Tell me, Hylas, when you behold the picture of Julius Caesar, do you see with your eyes any more than some colors and figures, with a certain symmetry and composition of the whole?

Hyl. Nothing else.

Phil. And would not a man who had never known anything of Julius Caesar see as much?

Hyl. He would.

Phil. Consequently, he has his sight and the use of it in as perfect a degree as you?

Hyl. I agree with you.

Phil. Whence comes it then that your thoughts are directed to the Roman emperor, and his are not? This cannot proceed from the sensations or ideas of sense by you then perceived, since you acknowledge you have no advantage over him in that respect. It should seem therefore to proceed from reason and memory, should it not?

Hyl. It should.

Phil. Consequently, it will not follow from that instance that anything is perceived by sense which is not immediately perceived. Though I grant we may, in one acceptation, be said to perceive sensible things mediately by sense—that is, when, from a frequently perceived connection, the immediate perception of ideas by one sense suggest to the mind others, perhaps belonging to another sense, which are wont to be connected with them. For instance, when I hear a coach drive along the streets, immediately I perceive only the sound; but from the experience I have had that such a sound is connected with a coach, I am said to hear the coach. It is nevertheless evident that, in truth and strictness, nothing can be *heard* but *sound;* and the coach is not then properly perceived by sense, but suggested from experience. So likewise when we are said to see a red-hot bar of iron; the solidity and heat of the iron are not the objects of sight, but suggested to the imagination by the color and figure which are properly perceived by that sense. In short, those things alone are actually and strictly perceived by any sense which would have been perceived in case that same sense had then been first conferred on us. As for other things, it is plain they are only suggested to the mind by experience grounded on former perceptions. But, to return to your comparison of Caesar's picture, it is plain, if you keep to that, you must hold the real things or archetypes of our ideas are not perceived by sense, but by some internal faculty of the soul, as reason or memory. I would, therefore, fain know what arguments you can draw from reason for the existence of what you call "real things" or "material objects," or whether you remember to have seen them formerly as they are in themselves, or if you have heard or read of anyone that did.

Hyl. I see, Philonous, you are disposed to raillery; but that will never convince me.

Phil. My aim is only to learn from you the way to come at the knowledge of "material beings." Whatever we perceive is perceived either immediately or mediately—by sense, or by reason and reflection. But, as you have excluded sense, pray show me what reason you have to believe their existence, or what *medium* you can possibly make use of to prove it, either to mine or your own understanding.

Hyl. To deal ingenuously, Philonous, now [that] I consider the point, I do not find I can give you any good reason for it. But this much seems pretty plain, that it is at least possible such things may really exist. And as long as there is no absurdity in supposing them, I am resolved to believe as I did, till you bring good reasons to the contrary.

Phil. What! is it come to this, that you only believe the existence of material objects, and that your belief is founded barely on the possibility of its being true? Then you will have me bring reasons against it, though another would think it reasonable the proof should lie on him who holds the affirmative. And, after all, this very point which you are now resolved to maintain, without any reason, is in effect what you have more than once during this discourse seen good reason to give up. But to pass over all this—if I understand you rightly, you say our ideas do not exist without the mind, but that they are copies, images, or representations of certain originals that do?

Hyl. You take me right.

Phil. They are then like external things?

Hyl. They are.

Phil. Have those things a stable and permanent nature, independent of our senses, or are they in a perpetual change, upon our producing any motions in our bodies, suspending, exerting, or altering our faculties or organs of sense?

Hyl. Real things, it is plain, have a fixed and real nature, which remains the same notwithstanding any change in our senses or in the posture and motion of our bodies; which indeed may affect the ideas in our minds, but it were absurd to think they had the same effect on things existing without the mind.

Phil. How then is it possible that things perpetually fleeting and variable as our ideas should be copies or images of anything fixed and constant? Or, in other words, since all sensible qualities, as size, figure, color, etc., that is, our ideas, are continually changing upon every alteration in the distance, medium, or instruments of sensation—how can any determinate material objects be properly represented or painted forth by several distinct things each of which is so different from and unlike the rest? Or, if you say it resembles some one only of our ideas, how shall we be able to distinguish the true copy from all the false ones?

Hyl. I profess, Philonous, I am at a loss. I know not what to say to this.

Phil. But neither is this all. Which are material objects in themselves—perceptible or imperceptible?

Hyl. Properly and immediately nothing can be perceived but ideas. All material things, therefore, are in themselves insensible and to be perceived only by their ideas.

Phil. Ideas then are sensible, and their archetypes or originals insensible?

Hyl. Right.

Phil. But how can that which is sensible be like that which is insensible? Can a real thing, in itself *invisible*, be like a *color*, or a real thing which is not *audible* be like a *sound*? In a word, can anything be like a sensation or idea, but another sensation or idea?

Hyl. I must own, I think not.

Phil. Is it possible there should be any doubt on the point? Do you not perfectly know your own ideas?

Hyl. I know them perfectly, since what I do not perceive or know can be no part of my idea.

Phil. Consider, therefore, and examine them, and then tell me if there be anything in them which can exist without the mind, or if you can conceive anything like them existing without the mind?

Hyl. Upon inquiry I find it is impossible for me to conceive or understand how anything but an idea can be like an idea. And it is most evident that *no idea can exist without the mind.*

Phil. You are, therefore, by your principles forced to deny the reality of sensible things, since you made it to consist in an absolute existence exterior to the mind. That is to say, you are a downright skeptic. So I have gained my point, which was to show your principles led to skepticism.

Hyl. For the present I am, if not entirely convinced, at least silenced.

Phil. I would fain know what more you would require in order to a perfect conviction. Have you not had the liberty of explaining yourself all manner of ways? Were any little slips in discourse laid hold and insisted on? Or were you not allowed to retract or reinforce anything you had offered, as best served your purpose? Has not everything you could say been heard and examined with all the fairness imaginable? In a word, have you not in every point been convinced out of your own mouth? And, if you can at present discover any flaw in any of your former concessions, or think of any remaining subterfuge, any new distinction, color, or comment whatsoever, why do you not produce it?

Hyl. A little patience, Philonous. I am at present so amazed to see myself ensnared, and as it were imprisoned in the labyrinths you have drawn me into, that on the sudden it cannot be expected I should find my way out. You must give me time to look about me and recollect myself.

Phil. Hark; is not this the college bell?

Hyl. It rings for prayers.

Phil. We will go in then, if you please, and meet here again tomorrow morning. In the meantime, you may employ your thoughts on this morning's discourse and try if you can find any fallacy in it, or invent any new means to extricate yourself.

Hyl. Agreed.

THE SECOND DIALOGUE

Hylas. I beg your pardon, Philonous, for not meeting you sooner. All this morning my head was so filled with our late conversation that I had not leisure to think of the time of the day, or indeed of anything else.

Philonous. I am glad you were so intent upon it, in hopes if there were any mistakes in your concessions, or fallacies in my reasonings from them, you will now discover them to me.

Hyl. I assure you I have done nothing ever since I saw you but search after mistakes and fallacies, and, with that [in] view, have minutely examined the whole series of yesterday's discourse; but all in vain, for the notions it led me into, upon review, appear still more clear and evident; and the more I consider them, the more irresistibly do they force my assent.

Phil. And is not this, think you, a sign that they are genuine, that they proceed from nature and are conformable to right reason? Truth and beauty are in this alike, that the strictest survey sets them both off to advantage, while the false luster of error and disguise cannot endure being reviewed or too nearly inspected.

Hyl. I own there is a great deal in what you say. Nor can anyone be more entirely satisfied of the truth of those odd consequences so long as I have in view the reasonings that lead to them. But when these are out of my thoughts, there seems, on the other hand, something so satisfactory, so natural and intelligible in the modern way of explaining things that I profess I know not how to reject it.

Phil. I know not what you mean.

Hyl. I mean the way of accounting for our sensations or ideas.

Phil. How is that?

Hyl. It is supposed the soul makes her residence in some part of the brain, from which the nerves take their rise, and

are thence extended to all parts of the body; and that outward objects, by the different impressions they make on the
organs of sense, communicate certain vibrative motions to
the nerves, and these, being filled with spirits, propagate them
to the brain or seat of the soul, which, according to the various
impressions or traces thereby made in the brain, is variously
affected with ideas.

Phil. And call you this an explication of the manner where-
by we are affected with ideas?

Hyl. Why not, Philonous; have you anything to object
against it?

Phil. I would first know whether I rightly understand your
hypothesis. You make certain traces in the brain to be the
causes or occasions of our ideas. Pray tell me whether by the
"brain" you mean any sensible thing.

Hyl. What else think you I could mean?

Phil. Sensible things are all immediately perceivable; and
those things which are immediately perceivable are ideas, and
these exist only in the mind. This much you have, if I mistake
not, long since agreed to.

Hyl. I do not deny it.

Phil. The brain therefore you speak of, being a sensible
thing, exists only in the mind. Now I would fain know whether
you think it reasonable to suppose that one idea or thing existing in the mind occasions all other ideas. And if you think so,
pray how do you account for the origin of that primary idea
or brain itself?

Hyl. I do not explain the origin of our ideas by that brain
which is perceivable to sense, this being itself only a combination of sensible ideas, but by another which I imagine.

Phil. But are not things imagined as truly *in the mind* as
things perceived?

Hyl. I must confess they are.

Phil. It comes, therefore, to the same thing; and you have
been all this while accounting for ideas by certain motions or
impressions of the brain, that is, by some alterations in an
idea, whether sensible or imaginable it matters not.

Hyl. I begin to suspect my hypothesis.

Phil. Besides spirits, all that we know or conceive are our own ideas. When, therefore, you say all ideas are occasioned by impressions in the brain, do you conceive this brain or no? If you do, then you talk of ideas imprinted in an idea causing that same idea, which is absurd. If you do not conceive it, you talk unintelligibly, instead of forming a reasonable hypothesis.

Hyl. I now clearly see it was a mere dream. There is nothing in it.

Phil. You need not be much concerned at it, for, after all, this way of explaining things, as you called it, could never have satisfied any reasonable man. What connection is there between a motion in the nerves and the sensations of sound or color in the mind? Or how is it possible these should be the effect of that?

Hyl. But I could never think it had so little in it as now it seems to have.

Phil. Well then, are you at length satisfied that no sensible things have a real existence, and that you are in truth an arrant *skeptic?*

Hyl. It is too plain to be denied.

Phil. Look! are not the fields covered with a delightful verdure? Is there not something in the woods and groves, in the rivers and clear springs, that soothes, that delights, that transports the soul? At the prospect of the wide and deep ocean, or some huge mountain whose top is lost in the clouds, or of an old gloomy forest, are not our minds filled with a pleasing horror? Even in rocks and deserts is there not an agreeable wildness? How sincere a pleasure is it to behold the natural beauties of the earth! To preserve and renew our relish for them, is not the veil of night alternately drawn over her face, and does she not change her dress with the seasons? How aptly are the elements disposed! What variety and use in the meanest productions of nature! What delicacy, what beauty, what contrivance in animal and vegetable bodies! How exquisitely are all things suited, as well to their particular ends as to constitute apposite parts of the whole! And while they mutually aid and support, do they not also set off and illustrate each other? Raise now your thoughts from this ball of earth to all those glorious luminaries that adorn the high arch of heaven. The motion and situation of the planets, are they not admirable for use and order? Were those (miscalled "erratic") globes ever known to stray in their repeated journeys through the pathless void? Do they not measure areas round the sun ever proportioned to the times? So fixed, so immutable are the laws by which the unseen Author of nature actuates the universe. How vivid and radiant is the luster of the fixed stars! How magnificent and rich that negligent profusion with which they appear to be scattered throughout the whole azure vault! Yet, if you take the telescope, it brings into your sight a new host of stars that escape the naked eye. Here they seem contiguous and minute, but to a nearer view, immense orbs of light at various distances, far sunk in the abyss of space. Now you must call imagination to your aid. The feeble narrow sense cannot descry innumerable worlds revolving round the central fires, and in those worlds the energy of an all-perfect Mind displayed in endless forms. But neither sense nor imagination are big enough to comprehend the boundless extent with all its glittering furniture. Though the laboring mind exert and strain each power to its utmost reach, there still stands out ungrasped a surplusage immeasurable. Yet all the vast bodies that compose this mighty frame, how distant and remote soever, are by some secret mechanism, some divine art and force linked in a mutual dependence and intercourse with each other, even with this earth, which was almost slipt from my thoughts and lost in the crowd of worlds. Is not the whole system immense, beautiful, glorious beyond expression and beyond thought! What treatment, then, do those philosophers deserve who would deprive these noble and delightful scenes of all reality? How should those principles be entertained that lead us to think all the visible beauty of the creation a false imaginary glare? To be plain, can you expect this skepticism of yours will not be thought extravagantly absurd by all men of sense?

Hyl. Other men may think as they please, but for your part you have nothing to reproach me with. My comfort is you are as much a skeptic as I am.

Phil. There, Hylas, I must beg leave to differ from you.

Hyl. What! have you all along agreed to the premises, and do you now deny the conclusion and leave me to maintain those paradoxes by myself which you led me into? This surely is not fair.

Phil. I deny that I agreed with you in those notions that led to skepticism. You indeed said the *reality* of sensible things consisted in an *absolute existence* out of the minds of spirits, or distinct from their being perceived. And, pursuant to this notion of reality, you are obliged to deny sensible things any real existence; that is, according to your own definition, you profess yourself a skeptic. But I neither said nor thought the reality of sensible things was to be defined after that manner. To me it is evident, for the reasons you allow of, that sensible things cannot exist otherwise than in a mind or spirit. Whence I conclude, not that they have no real existence, but that, seeing they depend not on my thought and have an existence distinct from being perceived by me, *there must be some other mind wherein they exist.* As sure, therefore, as the sensible world really exists, so sure is there an infinite omnipresent Spirit, who contains and supports it.

Hyl. What! this is no more than I and all Christians hold; nay, and all others, too, who believe there is a God and that He knows and comprehends all things.

Phil. Aye, but here lies the difference. Men commonly believe that all things are known or perceived by God, because they believe the being of a God; whereas I, on the other side, immediately and necessarily conclude the being of a God, because all sensible things must be perceived by him.

Hyl. But so long as we all believe the same thing, what matter is it how we come by that belief?

Phil. But neither do we agree in the same opinion. For philosophers, though they acknowledge all corporeal beings to be perceived by God, yet they attribute to them an absolute subsistence distinct from their being perceived by any mind whatever, which I do not. Besides, is there no difference between saying, *there is a God, therefore He perceives all things,* and saying, *sensible things do really exist; and if they really exist, they are necessarily perceived by an infinite mind: therefore there is an infinite mind, or God?* This furnishes you with a direct and immediate demonstration, from a most evident principle, of the *being of a God.* Divines and philosophers had proved beyond all controversy, from the beauty and usefulness of the several parts of the creation, that it was the workmanship of God. But that—setting aside all help of astronomy and natural philosophy, all contemplation of the contrivance, order and adjustment of things—an infinite mind should be necessarily inferred from the bare *existence* of the sensible world is an advantage peculiar to them only who have made this easy reflection, that the sensible world is that which we perceive by our several senses; and that nothing is perceived by the senses besides ideas; and that no idea or archetype of an idea can exist otherwise than in a mind. You may now, without any laborious search into the sciences, without any subtlety of reason or tedious length of discourse, oppose and baffle the most strenuous advocate for atheism, those miserable refuges, whether in an eternal succession of unthinking causes and effects or in a fortuitous concourse of atoms; those wild imaginations of Vanini, Hobbes, and Spinoza: in a word, the whole system of atheism, is it not entirely overthrown by this single reflection on the repugnancy included in supposing the whole or any part, even the most rude and shapeless, of the visible world to exist without a mind? Let any one of those abettors of impiety but look into his own thoughts, and there try if he can conceive how so much as a rock, a desert, a chaos, or confused jumble of atoms, how anything at all, either sensible or imaginable, can exist independent of a mind, and he need go no further to be convinced of his folly. Can anything be fairer than to put a dispute on such an issue and leave it to a man himself to see if he can conceive, even in thought, what he holds to be true in fact, and from a notional to allow it a real existence?

Hyl. It cannot be denied there is something highly serviceable to religion in what you advance. But do you not think it looks very like a notion entertained by some eminent moderns, of *seeing all things in God?*

Phil. I would gladly know that opinion; pray explain it to me.

Hyl. They conceive that the soul, being immaterial, is incapable of being united with material things so as to perceive them in themselves, but that she perceives them by her union with the substance of God, which, being spiritual, is therefore purely intelligible, or capable of being the immediate object of a spirit's thought. Besides, the divine essence contains in it perfections correspondent to each created being, and which are, for that reason, proper to exhibit or represent them to the mind.

Phil. I do not understand how our ideas, which are things altogether passive and inert, can be the essence or any part (or like any part) of the essence or substance of God, who is an impassive, indivisible, purely active being. Many more difficulties and objections there are which occur at first view against this hypothesis; but I shall only add that it is liable to all the absurdities of the common hypothesis, in making a created world exist otherwise than in the mind of a Spirit. Beside all which it has this peculiar to itself that it makes that material world serve to no purpose. And if it pass for a good argument against other hypotheses in the sciences that they suppose nature or the divine wisdom to make something in vain, or do that by tedious roundabout methods which might have been performed in a much more easy and compendious way, what shall we think of that hypothesis which supposes the whole world made in vain?

Hyl. But what say you, are not you too of opinion that we see all things in God? If I mistake not, what you advance comes near it.

Phil. [Few men think, yet all have opinions. Hence men's opinions are superficial and confused. It is nothing strange that tenets which in themselves are ever so different should nevertheless be confounded with each other by those who do not consider them attentively. I shall not therefore be surprised if some men imagine that I run into the enthusiasm of Malebranche, though in truth I am very remote from it. He builds on the most abstract general ideas, which I entirely disclaim. He asserts an absolute external world, which I deny. He maintains that we are deceived by our senses and know not the real natures or the true forms and figures of extended beings; of all which I hold the direct contrary. So that upon the whole there are no principles more fundamentally opposite than his and mine. It must be owned][1] I entirely agree with what the holy Scripture says, "That in God we live and move and have our being." But that we see things in His essence, after the manner above set forth, I am far from believing. Take here in brief my meaning: It is evident that the things I perceive are my own ideas, and that no idea can exist unless it be in a mind. Nor is it less plain that these ideas or things by me perceived, either themselves or their archetypes, exist independently of my mind; since I know myself not to be their author, it being out of my power to determine at pleasure what particular ideas I shall be affected with upon opening my eyes or ears. They must therefore exist in some other mind, whose will it is they should be exhibited to me. The things, I say, immediately perceived are ideas or sensations, call them which you will. But how can any idea or sensation exist in, or be produced by, anything but a mind or spirit? This indeed is inconceivable; and to assert that which is inconceivable is to talk nonsense, is it not?

Hyl. Without doubt.

---

1 The bracketed portion of this paragraph did not appear in the first and second editions.

Phil. But, on the other hand, it is very conceivable that they should exist in and be produced by a spirit, since this is no more than I daily experience in myself, inasmuch as I perceive numberless ideas, and, by an act of my will, can form a great variety of them and raise them up in my imagination; though, it must be confessed, these creatures of the fancy are not altogether so distinct, so strong, vivid, and permanent as those perceived by my senses, which latter are called "real things." From all which I conclude, *there is a Mind which affects me every moment with all the sensible impressions I perceive.* And from the variety, order, and manner of these I conclude the Author of them to be *wise, powerful, and good beyond comprehension.* Mark it well; I do not say I see things by perceiving that which represents them in the intelligible Substance of God. This I do not understand; but I say the things by me perceived are known by the understanding and produced by the will of an infinite Spirit. And is not all this most plain and evident? Is there any more in it than what a little observation of our own minds, and that which passes in them, not only enables us to conceive but also obliges us to acknowledge?

Hyl. I think I understand you very clearly and own the proof you give of a Deity seems no less evident than it is surprising. But allowing that God is the supreme and universal cause of all things, yet may there not be still a third nature besides spirits and ideas? May we not admit a subordinate and limited cause of our ideas? In a word, may there not for all that be *matter?*

Phil. How often must I inculcate the same thing? You allow the things immediately perceived by sense to exist nowhere without the mind; but there is nothing perceived by sense which is not perceived immediately: therefore there is nothing sensible that exists without the mind. The matter, therefore, which you still insist on is something intelligible, I suppose something that may be discovered by reason, and not by sense.

Hyl. You are in the right.

Phil. Pray let me know what reasoning your belief of matter is grounded on, and what this matter is in your present sense of it.

Hyl. I find myself affected with various ideas whereof I know I am not the cause; neither are they the cause of themselves or of one another, or capable of subsisting by themselves, as being altogether inactive, fleeting, dependent beings. They have therefore some cause distinct from me and them, of which I pretend to know no more than that it is *the cause of my ideas.* And this thing, whatever it be, I call "matter."

Phil. Tell me, Hylas, has everyone a liberty to change the current proper signification annexed to a common name in any language? For example, suppose a traveler should tell you that in a certain country men pass unhurt through the fire; and, upon explaining himself, you found he meant by the word "fire" that which others call "water"; or, if he should assert that there are trees that walk upon two legs, meaning men by the term "trees." Would you think this reasonable?

Hyl. No, I should think it very absurd. Common custom is the standard of propriety in language. And for any man to affect speaking improperly is to pervert the use of speech, and can never serve to a better purpose than to protract and multiply disputes where there is no difference in opinion.

Phil. And does not "matter," in the common current acceptation of the word, signify an extended, solid, movable, unthinking, inactive substance?

Hyl. It does.

Phil. And has it not been made evident that no such substance can possibly exist? And though it should be allowed to exist, yet how can that which is *inactive* be a *cause,* or that which is *unthinking* be a *cause of thought?* You may, indeed, if you please, annex to the word "matter" a contrary meaning to what is vulgarly received, and tell me you understand by it an unextended, thinking, active being which is the cause of our ideas. But what else is this than to play with words and run into that very fault you just now condemned with so much reason? I do by no means find fault with your reasoning, in that you collect a cause from the phenomena; but I deny that the cause deducible by reason can properly be termed "matter."

Hyl. There is indeed something in what you say. But I am afraid you do not thoroughly comprehend my meaning. I would by no means be thought to deny that God, or an infinite Spirit, is the Supreme Cause of all things. All I contend for is that, subordinate to the Supreme Agent, there is a cause of a limited and inferior nature which concurs in the production of our ideas, not by any act of will or spiritual efficiency, but by that kind of action which belongs to matter, *viz.*, motion.

Phil. I find you are at every turn relapsing into your old exploded conceit, of a movable and consequently an extended substance existing without the mind. What! have you already forgotten you were convinced, or are you willing I should repeat what has been said on that head? In truth, this is not fair dealing in you still to suppose the being of that which you have so often acknowledged to have no being. But, not to insist further on what has been so largely handled, I ask whether all your ideas are not perfectly passive and inert, including nothing of action in them.

Hyl. They are.

Phil. And are sensible qualities anything else but ideas?

Hyl. How often have I acknowledged that they are not.

Phil. But is not motion a sensible quality?

Hyl. It is.

Phil. Consequently, it is no action?

Hyl. I agree with you. And indeed it is very plain that when I stir my finger it remains passive, but my will which produced the motion is active.

Phil. Now I desire to know, in the first place, whether, motion being allowed to be no action, you can conceive any action besides volition; and, in the second place, whether to say something and conceive nothing be not to talk nonsense; and, lastly, whether, having considered the premises, you do not perceive that to suppose any efficient or active cause of our ideas other than *spirit* is highly absurd and unreasonable?

Hyl. I give up the point entirely. But, though matter may not be a cause, yet what hinders its being an *instrument* subservient to the Supreme Agent in the production of our ideas?

Phil. An instrument say you; pray what may be the figure, springs, wheels, and motions of that instrument?

Hyl. Those I pretend to determine nothing of, both the substance and its qualities being entirely unknown to me.

Phil. What! You are then of opinion it is made up of unknown parts, that it has unknown motions and an unknown shape?

Hyl. I do not believe that it has any figure or motion at all, being already convinced that no sensible qualities can exist in an unperceiving substance.

Phil. But what notion is it possible to frame of an instrument void of all sensible qualities, even extension itself?

Hyl. I do not pretend to have any notion of it.

Phil. And what reason have you to think this unknown, this inconceivable somewhat does exist? Is it that you imagine God cannot act as well without it, or that you find by experience the use of some such thing when you form ideas in your own mind?

Hyl. You are always teasing me for reasons of my belief. Pray what reasons have you not to believe it?

Phil. It is to me a sufficient reason not to believe the existence of anything if I see no reason for believing it. But, not to insist on reasons for believing, you will not so much as let me know what it is you would have me believe, since you say you have no manner of notion of it. After all, let me entreat you to consider whether it be like a philosopher, or even like a man of common sense, to pretend to believe you know not what, and you know not why.

Hyl. Hold, Philonous. When I tell you matter is an *instrument,* I do not mean altogether nothing. It is true I know not the particular kind of instrument, but, however, I have some notion of *instrument in general,* which I apply to it.

Phil. But what if it should prove that there is something, even in the most general notion of *instrument,* as taken in a distinct sense from *cause,* which makes the use of it inconsistent with the divine attributes?

Hyl. Make that appear and I shall give up the point.

Phil. What mean you by the general nature or notion of instrument?

Hyl. That which is common to all particular instruments composes the general notion.

Phil. Is it not common to all instruments that they are applied to the doing those things only which cannot be performed by the mere act of our wills? Thus, for instance, I never use an instrument to move my finger, because it is done by a volition. But I should use one if I were to remove part of a rock or tear up a tree by the roots. Are you of the same mind? Or can you show any example where an instrument is made use of in producing an effect immediately depending on the will of the agent?

Hyl. I own I cannot.

Phil. How, therefore, can you suppose that an all-perfect Spirit, on whose will all things have an absolute and immediate dependence, should need an instrument in his operations or, not needing it, make use of it? Thus it seems to me that you are obliged to own the use of a lifeless inactive instrument to be incompatible with the infinite perfection of God, that is, by your own confession, to give up the point.

Hyl. It does not readily occur what I can answer you.

Phil. But methinks you should be ready to own the truth when it has been fairly proved to you. We, indeed, who are beings of finite powers, are forced to make use of instruments. And the use of an instrument shows the agent to be limited by rules of another's prescription, and that he cannot obtain his end but in such a way and by such conditions. Whence it seems a clear consequence that the Supreme Unlimited Agent uses no tool or instrument at all. The will of an Omnipotent Spirit is no sooner exerted than executed, without the application of means, which, if they are employed by inferior agents, it is not upon account of any real efficacy that is in them, or necessary aptitude to produce any effect, but merely in compliance with the laws of nature or those conditions prescribed to them by the First Cause, who is Himself above all limitation or prescription whatsoever.

Hyl. I will no longer maintain that matter is an instrument. However, I would not be understood to give up its existence neither, since, notwithstanding what has been said, it may still be an *occasion*.

Phil. How many shapes is your matter to take? Or how often must it be proved not to exist before you are content to part with it? But to say no more of this (though by all the laws of disputation I may justly blame you for so frequently changing the signification of the principal term), I would fain know what you mean by affirming that matter is an "occasion," having already denied it to be a cause. And when you have shown in what sense you understand occasion, pray, in the next place, be pleased to show me what reason induces you to believe there is such an occasion of our ideas?

Hyl. As to the first point: by "occasion" I mean an inactive unthinking being, at the presence whereof God excites ideas in our minds.

Phil. And what may be the nature of that inactive unthinking being?

Hyl. I know nothing of its nature.

Phil. Proceed then to the second point and assign some reason why we should allow an existence to this inactive, unthinking, unknown thing.

Hyl. When we see ideas produced in our minds after an orderly and constant manner, it is natural to think they have some fixed and regular occasions at the presence of which they are excited.

Phil. You acknowledge then God alone to be the cause of our ideas, and that He causes them at the presence of those occasions.

Hyl. That is my opinion.

Phil. Those things which you say are present to God, without doubt He perceives.

Hyl. Certainly; otherwise they could not be to Him an occasion of acting.

Phil. Not to insist now on your making sense of this hypothesis, or answering all the puzzling questions and difficulties it is liable to: I only ask whether the order and regularity observable in the series of our ideas, or the course of nature, be not sufficiently accounted for by the wisdom and power of God; and whether it does not derogate from those attributes to suppose He is influenced, directed, or put in mind, when and what He is to act, by an unthinking substance? And, lastly, whether, in case I granted all you contend for, it would make anything to your purpose, it not being easy to conceive how the external or absolute existence of an unthinking substance, distinct from its being perceived, can be- inferred from my allowing that there are certain things perceived by the mind of God which are to Him the occasion of producing ideas in us?

Hyl. I am perfectly at a loss what to think, this notion of occasion seeming now altogether as groundless as the rest.

Phil. Do you not at length perceive that in all these different acceptations of matter you have been only supposing you know not what, for no manner of reason and to no kind of use?

Hyl. I freely own myself less fond of my notions since they have been so accurately examined. But still, methinks, I have some confused perception that there is such a thing as matter.

Phil. Either you perceive the being of matter immediately or mediately. If immediately, pray inform me by which of the senses you perceive it. If mediately, let me know by what reasoning it is inferred from those things which you perceive immediately. So much for the perception. Then for the matter itself, I ask whether it is object, substratum, cause, instrument, or occasion? You have already pleaded for each of these, shifting your notions and making matter to appear sometimes in one shape, then in another. And what you have offered has been disapproved and rejected by yourself. If you have anything new to advance I would gladly hear it.

Hyl. I think I have already offered all I had to say on those heads. I am at a loss what more to urge.

Phil. And yet you are loath to part with your old prejudice. But to make you quit it more easily, I desire that, besides what has been hitherto suggested, you will further consider whether, upon supposition that matter exists, you can possibly conceive how you should be affected by it? Or, supposing it did not exist, whether it be not evident you might for all that be affected with the same ideas you now are, and consequently have the very same reason to believe its existence that you now can have?

Hyl. I acknowledge it is possible we might perceive all things just as we do now, though there was no matter in the world; neither can I conceive, if there be matter, how it should produce any idea in our minds. And I do further grant you have entirely satisfied me that it is impossible there should be such a thing as matter in any of the foregoing acceptations. But still I cannot help supposing that there is *matter* in some sense or other. What that is I do not indeed pretend to determine.

Phil. I do not expect you should define exactly the nature of that unknown being. Only be pleased to tell me whether it is a substance—and if so, whether you can suppose a substance without accidents; or in case you suppose it to have accidents or qualities, I desire you will let me know what those qualities are, at least what is meant by "matter's supporting them?"

Hyl. We have already argued on those points. I have no more to say to them. But, to prevent any further questions, let me tell you I at present understand by "matter" neither substance nor accident, thinking nor extended being, neither cause, instrument, nor occasion, but something entirely unknown, distinct from all these.

Phil. It seems then you include in your present notion of matter nothing but the general abstract idea of *entity*.

Hyl. Nothing else, save only that I superadd to this general idea the negation of all those particular things, qualities, or ideas that I perceive, imagine, or in anywise apprehend.

Phil. Pray where do you suppose this unknown matter to exist?

Hyl. Oh Philonous! now you think you have entangled me; for if I say it exists in place, then you will infer that it exists in the mind, since it is agreed that place or extension exists only in the mind; but I am not ashamed to own my ignorance. I know not where it exists; only I am sure it exists not in place. There is a negative answer for you. And you must expect no other to all the questions you put for the future about matter.

Phil. Since you will not tell me where it exists, be pleased to inform me after what manner you suppose it to exist, or what you mean by its "existence?"

Hyl. It neither thinks nor acts, neither perceives nor is perceived.

Phil. But what is there positive in your abstracted notion of its existence?

Hyl. Upon a nice observation, I do not find I have any positive notion or meaning at all. I tell you again, I am not ashamed to own my ignorance. I know not what is meant by its existence or how it exists.

Phil. Continue, good Hylas, to act the same ingenuous part and tell me sincerely whether you can frame a distinct idea of entity in general, prescinded from and exclusive of all thinking and corporeal beings, all particular things whatsoever.

Hyl. Hold, let me think a little—— I profess, Philonous, I do not find that I can. At first glance methought I had some dilute and airy notion of pure entity in abstract, but, upon closer attention, it has quite vanished out of sight. The more I think on it, the more am I confirmed in my prudent reso-

lution of giving none but negative answers and not pretending to the least degree of any positive knowledge or conception of matter, its *where*, its *how*, its *entity*, or anything belonging to it.

Phil. When, therefore, you speak of the existence of matter, you have not any notion in your mind?

Hyl. None at all.

Phil. Pray tell me if the case stands not thus: at first, from
a belief of material substance, you would have it that the immediate objects existed without the mind; then, that they are
archetypes; then, causes; next, instruments; then, occasions:
lastly, *something in general*, which being interpreted proves
nothing. So matter comes to nothing. What think you, Hylas,
is not this a fair summary of your whole proceeding?

Hyl. Be that as it will, yet I still insist upon it, that our
not being able to conceive a thing is no argument against its
existence.

Phil. That from a cause, effect, operation, sign, or other
circumstance there may reasonably be inferred the existence of a thing not immediately perceived; and that it were
absurd for any man to argue against the existence of that
thing, from his having no direct and positive notion of it, I
freely own. But where there is nothing of all this, where
neither reason nor revelation induces us to believe the existence of a thing, where we have not even a relative notion of
it, where an abstraction is made from perceiving and being
perceived, from spirit and idea, lastly, where there is not
so much as the most inadequate or faint idea pretended to,
I will not, indeed, thence conclude against the reality of any
notion or existence of anything; but my inference shall be
that you mean nothing at all, that you employ words to no
manner of purpose, without any design or signification whatsoever. And I leave it to you to consider how mere jargon
should be treated.

Hyl. To deal frankly with you, Philonous, your arguments
seem in themselves unanswerable, but they have not so great

an effect on me as to produce that entire conviction, that hearty acquiescence, which attends demonstration. I find myself still relapsing into an obscure surmise of I know not what —*matter*.

Phil. But are you not sensible, Hylas, that two things must concur to take away all scruple and work a plenary assent in the mind? Let a visible object be set in never so clear a light, yet, if there is any imperfection in the sight, or if the eye is not directed toward it, it will not be distinctly seen. And though a demonstration be never so well grounded and fairly proposed, yet, if there is withal a stain of prejudice or a wrong bias on the understanding, can it be expected on a sudden to perceive clearly and adhere firmly to the truth? No, there is need of time and pains: the attention must be awakened and detained by a frequent repetition of the same thing placed oft in the same, oft in different lights. I have said it already, and find I must still repeat and inculcate, that it is an unaccountable license you take in pretending to maintain you know not what, for you know not what reason, to you know not what purpose. Can this be paralleled in any art or science, any sect or profession of men? Or is there anything so barefacedly groundless and unreasonable to be met with even in the lowest of common conversation? But, perhaps, you will still say, matter may exist, though at the same time you neither know what is meant by "matter" or by its "existence." This indeed is surprising, and the more so because it is altogether voluntary, you not being led to it by any one reason, for I challenge you to show me that thing in nature which needs matter to explain or account for it.

Hyl. The reality of things cannot be maintained without supposing the existence of matter. And is not this, think you, a good reason why I should be earnest in its defense?

Phil. The reality of things! What things, sensible or intelligible?

Hyl. Sensible things.

Phil. My glove, for example?

Hyl. That or any other thing perceived by the senses.

Phil. But to fix on some particular thing, is it not a sufficient evidence to me of the existence of this *glove* that I see it and feel it and wear it? Or, if this will not do, how is it possible I should be assured of the reality of this thing which I actually see in this place by supposing that some unknown thing, which I never did or can see, exists after an unknown manner, in an unknown place, or in no place at all? How can the supposed reality of that which is intangible be a proof that anything tangible really exists? Or of that which is invisible, that any visible thing or, in general, of anything which is imperceptible, that a perceptible exists? Do but explain this and I shall think nothing too hard for you.

Hyl. Upon the whole, I am content to own the existence of matter is highly improbable; but the direct and absolute impossibility of it does not appear to me.

Phil. But granting matter to be possible, yet, upon that account merely, it can have no more claim to existence than a golden mountain or a centaur.

Hyl. I acknowledge it, but still you do not deny it is possible; and that which is possible, for aught you know, may actually exist.

Phil. I deny it to be possible; and have, if I mistake not, evidently proved, from your own concessions, that it is not. In the common sense of the word "matter," is there any more implied than an extended, solid, figured, movable substance existing without the mind? And have not you acknowledged, over and over, that you have seen evident reason for denying the possibility of such a substance?

Hyl. True, but that is only one sense of the term "matter."

Phil. But is it not the only proper genuine received sense? And if matter in such a sense be proved impossible, may it not be thought with good grounds absolutely impossible? Else how could anything be proved impossible? Or, indeed, how could there be any proof at all one way or other to a man who takes the liberty to unsettle and change the common signification of words?

Hyl. I thought philosophers might be allowed to speak more accurately than the vulgar, and were not always confined to the common acceptation of a term.

Phil. But this now mentioned is the common received sense among philosophers themselves. But, not to insist on that, have you not been allowed to take matter in what sense you pleased? And have you not used this privilege in the utmost extent, sometimes entirely changing, at others leaving out or putting into the definition of it whatever, for the present, best served your design, contrary to all the known rules of reason and logic? And has not this shifting, unfair method of yours spun out our dispute to an unnecessary length, matter having been particularly examined and by your own confession refuted in each of those senses? And can any more be required to prove the absolute impossibility of a thing than the proving it impossible in every particular sense that either you or anyone else understands it in?

Hyl. But I am not so thoroughly satisfied that you have proved the impossibility of matter in the last most obscure abstracted and indefinite sense.

Phil. When is a thing shown to be impossible?

Hyl. When a repugnancy is demonstrated between the ideas comprehended in its definition.

Phil. But where there are no ideas, there no repugnancy can be demonstrated between ideas?

Hyl. I agree with you.

Phil. Now, in that which you call the obscure indefinite sense of the word "matter," it is plain, by your own confession, there was included no idea at all, no sense except an unknown sense, which is the same thing as none. You are not, therefore, to expect I should prove a repugnancy between ideas where there are no ideas, or the impossibility of matter taken in an *unknown* sense, that is, no sense at all. My business was only to show you meant *nothing;* and this you were brought to own. So that, in all your various senses, you have been shown either to mean nothing at all or, if anything, an absurdity. And if this be not sufficient to prove the impossibility of a thing, I desire you will let me know what is.

Hyl. I acknowledge you have proved that matter is impossible, nor do I see what more can be said in defense of it. But, at the same time that I give up this, I suspect all my other notions. For surely none could be more seemingly evident than this once was; and yet it now seems as false and absurd as ever it did true before. But I think we have discussed the point sufficiently for the present. The remaining part of the day I would willingly spend in running over in my thoughts the several heads of this morning's conversation, and tomorrow shall be glad to meet you here again about the same time.

Phil. I will not fail to attend you.

THE THIRD DIALOGUE

Philonous. Tell me, Hylas, what are the fruits of yesterday's meditation? Has it confirmed you in the same mind you were in at parting, or have you since seen cause to change your opinion?

Hylas. Truly my opinion is that all our opinions are alike vain and uncertain. What we approve today, we condemn tomorrow. We keep a stir about knowledge and spend our lives in the pursuit of it, when, alas! we know nothing all the while; nor do I think it possible for us ever to know anything in this life. Our faculties are too narrow and too few. Nature certainly never intended us for speculation.

Phil. What! say you we can know nothing, Hylas?

Hyl. There is not that single thing in the world whereof we can know the real nature, or what it is in itself.

Phil. Will you tell me I do not really know what fire or water is?

Hyl. You may indeed know that fire appears hot, and water fluid; but this is no more than knowing what sensations are produced in your own mind upon the application of fire and water to your organs of sense. Their internal constitution, their true and real nature, you are utterly in the dark as to *that*.

Phil. Do I not know this to be a real stone that I stand on, and that which I see before my eyes to be a real tree?

Hyl. Know? No, it is impossible you or any man alive should know it. All you know is that you have such a certain idea or appearance in your own mind. But what is this to the real tree or stone? I tell you that color, figure, and hardness, which you perceive, are not the real natures of those things, or in the least like them. The same may be said of all other real things or corporeal substances which compose the world. They have, none of them, anything in themselves, like

those sensible qualities by us perceived. We should not, therefore, pretend to affirm or know anything of them, as they
are in their own nature.

Phil. But surely, Hylas, I can distinguish gold, for example,
from iron; and how could this be if I knew not what either
truly was?

Hyl. Believe me, Philonous, you can only distinguish between your own ideas. That yellowness, that weight, and other
sensible qualities, think you they are really in the gold? They
are only relative to the senses and have no absolute existence
in nature. And in pretending to distinguish the species of real
things by the appearances in your mind, you may perhaps act
as wisely as he that should conclude two men were of a different species because their clothes were not of the same color.

Phil. It seems, then, we are altogether put off with the ap-
pearances of things, and those false ones, too. The very meat
I eat, and the cloth I wear, have nothing in them like what
I see and feel.

Hyl. Even so.

Phil. But is it not strange the whole world should be thus
imposed on and so foolish as to believe their senses? And yet
I know not how it is, but men eat, and drink, and sleep, and
perform all the offices of life as comfortably and conveniently
as if they really knew the things they are conversant about.

Hyl. They do so; but you know ordinary practice does not
require a nicety of speculative knowledge. Hence the vulgar
retain their mistakes, and for all that make a shift to bustle
through the affairs of life. But philosophers know better
things.

Phil. You mean they know that they *know nothing*.

Hyl. That is the very top and perfection of human knowledge.

Phil. But are you all this while in earnest, Hylas; and are
you seriously persuaded that you know nothing real in the
world? Suppose you are going to write, would you not call
for pen, ink, and paper, like another man; and do you not
know what it is you call for?

Hyl. How often must I tell you that I know not the real nature of any one thing in the universe? I may indeed upon occasion make use of pen, ink, and paper. But what any one of them is in its own true nature, I declare positively I know not. And the same is true with regard to every other corporeal thing. And what is more, we are not only ignorant of the true and real nature of things, but even of their existence. It cannot be denied that we perceive such certain appearances or ideas, but it cannot be concluded from thence that bodies really exist. Nay, now I think on it, I must, agreeably to my former concessions, further declare that it is impossible any real corporeal thing should exist in nature.

Phil. You amaze me. Was ever anything more wild and extravagant than the notions you now maintain? And is it not evident you are led into all these extravagances by the belief of *material substance?* This makes you dream of those unknown natures in everything. It is this occasions your distinguishing between the reality and sensible appearances of things. It is to this you are indebted for being ignorant of what everybody else knows perfectly well. Nor is this all: you are not only ignorant of the true nature of everything, but you know not whether any thing really exists or whether there are any true natures at all, forasmuch as you attribute to your material beings an absolute or external existence wherein you suppose their reality consists. And as you are forced in the end to acknowledge such an existence means either a direct repugnancy or nothing at all, it follows that you are obliged to pull down your own hypothesis of material substance and positively to deny the real existence of any part of the universe. And so you are plunged into the deepest and most deplorable skepticism that ever man was. Tell me, Hylas, is it not as I say?

Hyl. I agree with you. "Material substance" was no more than a hypothesis, and a false and groundless one, too. I will no longer spend my breath in defense of it. But whatever hypothesis you advance or whatsoever scheme of things you introduce in its stead, I doubt not it will appear every whit as false; let me but be allowed to question you upon it. That is, suffer me to serve you in your own kind, and I warrant it shall conduct you through as many perplexities and contradictions to the very same state of skepticism that I myself am in at present.

Phil. I assure you, Hylas, I do not pretend to frame any hypothesis at all. I am of a vulgar cast, simple enough to believe my senses and leave things as I find them. To be plain, it is my opinion that the real things are those very things I see and feel, and perceive by my senses. These I know and, finding they answer all the necessities and purposes of life, have no reason to be solicitous about any other unknown beings. A piece of sensible bread, for instance, would stay my stomach better than ten thousand times as much of that insensible, unintelligible real bread you speak of. It is likewise my opinion that colors and other sensible qualities are on the objects. I cannot for my life help thinking that snow is white, and fire hot. You, indeed, who by "snow" and "fire" mean certain external, unperceived, unperceiving substances are in the right to deny whiteness or heat to be affections inherent in them. But I who understand by those words the things I see and feel am obliged to think like other folks. And as I am no skeptic with regard to the nature of things, so neither am I as to their existence. That a thing should be really perceived by my senses and at the same time not really exist is to me a plain contradiction, since I cannot prescind or abstract, even in thought, the existence of a sensible thing from its being perceived. Wood, stones, fire, water, flesh, iron, and the like things which I name and discourse of are things that I know. And I should not have known them but that I perceived them by my senses; and things perceived by the senses are immediately perceived; and things immediately perceived are ideas; and ideas cannot exist without the mind; their existence therefore consists in being perceived; when, therefore, they are actually perceived, there can be no doubt of their existence. Away then with all that skepticism, all those ridiculous philosophical doubts. What a jest is it for a philosopher to question the existence of sensible things till he has it proved to him from the veracity of God, or to pretend our knowledge in this point falls short of intuition or demonstration! I might as well doubt of my own being as of the being of those things I actually see and feel.

Hyl. Not so fast, Philonous: You say you cannot conceive how sensible things should exist without the mind. Do you not?

Phil. I do.

Hyl. Supposing you were annihilated, cannot you conceive it possible that things perceivable by sense may still exist?

Phil. I can, but then it must be in another mind. When I deny sensible things an existence out of the mind, I do not mean my mind in particular, but all minds. Now it is plain they have an existence exterior to my mind, since I find them by experience to be independent of it. There is therefore some other mind wherein they exist during the intervals between the times of my perceiving them, as likewise they did before my birth, and would do after my supposed annihilation. And as the same is true with regard to all other finite created spirits, it necessarily follows there is an *omnipresent eternal Mind* which knows and comprehends all things, and exhibits them to our view in such a manner and according to such rules as He Himself has ordained and are by us termed the "laws of nature."

Hyl. Answer me, Philonous. Are all our ideas perfectly inert beings? Or have they any agency included in them?

Phil. They are altogether passive and inert.

Hyl. And is not God an agent, a being purely active?

Phil. I acknowledge it.

Hyl. No idea, therefore, can be like unto or represent the nature of God.

Phil. It cannot.

Hyl. Since, therefore, you have no idea of the mind of God, how can you conceive it possible that things should exist in His mind? Or, if you can conceive the mind of God without having an idea of it, why may not I be allowed to conceive the existence of matter, notwithstanding I have no idea of it?

Phil. As to your first question: I own I have properly no *idea* either of God or any other spirit; for these, being active, cannot be represented by things perfectly inert as our ideas are. I do nevertheless know that I, who am a spirit or thinking substance, exist as certainly as I know my ideas exist. Further, I know what I mean by the terms "I" and "myself"; and I know this immediately or intuitively, though I do not perceive it as I perceive a triangle, a color, or a sound. The mind, spirit, or soul is that indivisible unextended thing which thinks, acts, and perceives. I say "indivisible," because unextended; and "unextended," because extended, figured, movable things are ideas; and that which perceives ideas, which thinks and wills, is plainly itself no idea, nor like an idea. Ideas are things inactive and perceived. And spirits a sort of beings altogether different from them. I do not therefore say my soul is an idea, or like an idea. However, taking the word "idea" in a large sense, my soul may be said to furnish me with an idea, that is, an image or likeness of God, though indeed extremely inadequate. For all the notion I have of God is obtained by reflecting on my own soul, heightening its powers, and removing its imperfections. I have, therefore, though not an inactive idea, yet in *myself* some sort of an active thinking image of the Deity. And though I perceive Him not by sense, yet I have a notion of Him, or know Him by reflection and reasoning. My own mind and my own ideas I have an immediate knowledge of; and, by the help of these, do mediately apprehend the possibility of the existence of other spirits and ideas. Further, from my own being, and from the dependency I find in myself and my ideas, I do, by an act of reason, necessarily infer the existence of a God and of all created things in the mind of God. So much for your first question. For the second: I suppose by this time you can answer it yourself. For you neither perceive matter objectively, as you do an inactive being or idea, nor know it, as you do yourself by a reflex act; neither do you mediately apprehend it by similitude of the one or the other, nor yet collect it by reasoning from that which you know immediately. All which makes the case of *matter* widely different from that of the *Deity.*

[*Hyl.*[1] You say your own soul supplies you with some sort of an idea or image of God. But, at the same time, you acknowledge you have, properly speaking, no idea of your own soul. You even affirm that spirits are a sort of beings altogether different from ideas. Consequently, that no idea can be like a spirit. We have, therefore, no idea of any spirit. You admit nevertheless that there is spiritual substance, although you have no idea of it, while you deny there can be such a thing as material substance, because you have no notion or idea of it. Is this fair dealing? To act consistently, you must either admit matter or reject spirit. What say you to this?

Phil. I say, in the first place, that I do not deny the existence of material substance merely because I have no notion of it, but because the notion of it is inconsistent, or, in other words, because it is repugnant that there should be a notion of it. Many things, for aught I know, may exist whereof neither I nor any other man has or can have any idea or notion whatsoever. But then those things must be possible, that is, nothing inconsistent must be included in their definition. I say, secondly, that, although we believe things to exist which we do not perceive, yet we may not believe that any particular thing exists without some reason for such belief; but I have no reason for believing the existence of matter. I have no immediate intuition thereof, neither can I immediately from my sensations, ideas, notions, actions, or passions infer an unthinking, unperceiving, inactive substance, either by probable deduction or necessary consequence. Whereas the being of my self, that is, my own soul, mind, or thinking principle, I evidently know by reflection. You will forgive me if I repeat the same things in answer to the same objections. In the very notion or definition of "material substance" there is included a manifest repugnance and inconsistency. But this cannot be

[1] The four paragraphs following do not appear in the first and second editions.

said of the notion of spirit. That ideas should exist in what does not perceive, or be produced by what does not act, is repugnant. But it is no repugnancy to say that a perceiving thing should be the subject of ideas, or an active thing the cause of them. It is granted we have neither an immediate evidence nor a demonstrative knowledge of the existence of other finite spirits, but it will not thence follow that such spirits are on a foot with material substances, if to suppose the one be inconsistent, and it be not inconsistent to suppose the other; if the one can be inferred by no argument, and there is a probability for the other; if we see signs and effects indicating distinct finite agents like ourselves, and see no sign or symptom whatever that leads to a rational belief of matter. I say, lastly, that I have a notion of spirit, though I have not, strictly speaking, an idea of it. I do not perceive it as an idea, or by means of an idea, but know it by reflection.

Hyl. Notwithstanding all you have said, to me it seems that, according to your own way of thinking, and in consequence of your own principles, it should follow that you are only a system of floating ideas without any substance to support them. Words are not to be used without a meaning. And, as there is no more meaning in *spiritual* substance than in *material* substance, the one is to be exploded as well as the other.

Phil. How often must I repeat that I know or am conscious of my own being, and that *I myself* am not my ideas, but somewhat else, a thinking, active principle that perceives, knows, wills, and operates about ideas. I know that I, one and the same self, perceive both colors and sounds, that a color cannot perceive a sound, nor a sound a color, that I am therefore one individual principle distinct from color and sound, and, for the same reason, from all other sensible things and inert ideas. But I am not in like manner conscious either of the existence or essence of matter. On the contrary, I know that nothing inconsistent can exist, and that the existence of matter implies an inconsistency. Further, I know what I mean when I affirm that there is a spiritual substance or support of ideas, that is, that a spirit knows and perceives ideas. But I do not know what is meant when it is said that an unperceiving substance has inherent in it and supports either ideas or the archetypes of ideas. There is, therefore, upon the whole no parity of case between spirit and matter.]

Hyl. I own myself satisfied in this point. But do you in earnest think the real existence of sensible things consists in their being actually perceived? If so, how comes it that all mankind distinguish between them? Ask the first man you meet, and he shall tell you, "to be perceived" is one thing, and "to exist" is another.

Phil. I am content, Hylas, to appeal to the common sense of the world for the truth of my notion. Ask the gardener why he thinks yonder cherry tree exists in the garden, and he shall tell you, because he sees and feels it; in a word, because he perceives it by his senses. Ask him why he thinks an orange tree not to be there, and he shall tell you, because he does not perceive it. What he perceives by sense, that he terms a real being and says it "is" or "exists"; but that which is not perceivable, the same, he says, has no being.

Hyl. Yes, Philonous, I grant the existence of a sensible thing consists in being perceivable, but not in being actually perceived.

Phil. And what is perceivable but an idea? And can an idea exist without being actually perceived? These are points long since agreed between us.

Hyl. But be your opinion never so true, yet surely you will not deny it is shocking and contrary to the common sense of men. Ask the fellow whether yonder tree has an existence out of his mind; what answer think you he would make?

Phil. The same that I should myself, to wit, that it does exist out of his mind. But then to a Christian it cannot surely be shocking to say, the real tree, existing without his mind, is truly known and comprehended by (that is, *exists in*) the infinite mind of God. Probably he may not at first glance be aware of the direct and immediate proof there is of this, inasmuch as the very being of a tree, or any other sensible thing, implies a mind wherein it is. But the point itself he cannot deny. The question between the materialists and me is not whether things have a *real* existence out of the mind of this or that person, but, whether they have an *absolute* existence, distinct from being perceived by God, and exterior to all minds. This, indeed, some heathens and philosophers have affirmed, but whoever entertains notions of the Deity suitable to the Holy Scriptures will be of another opinion.

Hyl. But, according to your notions, what difference is there between real things and chimeras formed by the imagination or the visions of a dream, since they are all equally in the mind?

Phil. The ideas formed by the imagination are faint and indistinct; they have, besides, an entire dependence on the will. But the ideas perceived by sense, that is, real things, are more vivid and clear, and, being imprinted on the mind by a spirit distinct from us, have not the like dependence on our will. There is, therefore, no danger of confounding these with the foregoing, and there is as little of confounding them with the visions of a dream, which are dim, irregular, and confused. And though they should happen to be never so lively and natural, yet, by their not being connected and of a piece with the preceding and subsequent transaction of our lives, they might easily be distinguished from realities. In short, by whatever method you distinguish *things* from *chimeras* on your own scheme, the same, it is evident, will hold also upon mine. For it must be, I presume, by some perceived difference, and I am not for depriving you of any one thing that you perceive.

Hyl. But still, Philonous, you hold there is nothing in the world but spirits and ideas. And this you must needs acknowledge sounds very oddly.

Phil. I own the word "idea," not being commonly used for "thing," sounds something out of the way. My reason for using it was because a necessary relation to the mind is understood to be implied by the term; and it is now commonly used by philosophers to denote the immediate objects of the understanding. But however oddly the proposition may sound in words, yet it includes nothing so very strange or shocking in its sense, which in effect amounts to no more than this, to wit, that there are only things perceiving and things perceived, or that every unthinking being is necessarily, and from the very nature of its existence, perceived by some mind, if not by any finite created mind, yet certainly by the infinite mind of God, in whom "we live, and move, and have our being." Is this as strange as to say the sensible qualities are not on the object or that we cannot be sure of the existence of things, or know anything of their real natures, though we both see and feel them and perceive them by all our senses?

Hyl. And, in consequence of this, must we not think there are no such things as physical or corporeal causes, but that a spirit is the immediate cause of all the *phenomena* in nature? Can there be anything more extravagant than this?

Phil. Yes, it is infinitely more extravagant to say a thing which is inert operates on the mind, and which is unperceiving is the cause of our perceptions. Besides, that which to you I know not for what reason seems so extravagant is no more than the Holy Scriptures assert in a hundred places. In them God is represented as the sole and immediate Author of all those effects which some heathens and philosophers are wont to ascribe to Nature, Matter, Fate, or the like unthinking principle. This is so much the constant language of Scripture that it were needless to confirm it by citations.

Hyl. You are not aware, Philonous, that, in making God the immediate Author of all the motions in nature, you make Him the Author of murder, sacrilege, adultery, and the like heinous sins.

Phil. In answer to that I observe, first, that the imputation of guilt is the same whether a person commits an action with or without an instrument. In case, therefore, you suppose God to act by the mediation of an instrument or occasion called "matter," you as truly make Him the author of sin as I, who think Him the immediate agent in all those operations vulgarly ascribed to Nature. I further observe that sin or moral turpitude does not consist in the outward physical action or motion, but in the internal deviation of the will from the laws of reason and religion. This is plain, in that the killing an enemy in a battle or putting a criminal legally to death is not thought sinful, though the outward act be the very same with that in the case of murder. Since, therefore, sin does not consist in the physical action, the making God an immediate cause of all such actions is not making Him the Author of sin. Lastly, I have nowhere said that God is the only agent who produces all the motions in bodies. It is true I have denied there are any other agents besides spirits, but this is very consistent with allowing to thinking rational beings, in the production of motions, the use of limited powers, ultimately, indeed, derived from God but immediately under the direction of their own wills, which is sufficient to entitle them to all the guilt of their actions.

Hyl. But the denying matter, Philonous, or corporeal substance, there is the point. You can never persuade me that this is not repugnant to the universal sense of mankind. Were our dispute to be determined by most voices, I am confident you would give up the point without gathering the votes.

Phil. I wish both our opinions were fairly stated and submitted to the judgment of men who had plain common sense, without the prejudices of a learned education. Let me be represented as one who trusts his senses, who thinks he knows the things he sees and feels, and entertains no doubts of their existence; and you fairly set forth with all your doubts, your paradoxes, and your skepticism about you, and I shall willingly acquiesce in the determination of any indifferent person. That there is no substance wherein ideas can exist besides spirit is to me evident. And that the objects immediately perceived are ideas is on all hands agreed. And that sensible qualities are objects immediately perceived no one can deny. It is therefore evident there can be no *substratum* of those qualities but spirit, in which they exist, not by way of mode or property, but as a thing perceived in that which perceives it. I deny, therefore, that there is any unthinking *substratum* of the objects of sense, and in that acceptation that there is any material substance. But if by "material substance" is meant

only sensible body, that which is seen and felt (and the unphilosophical part of the world, I dare say, mean no more),
then I am more certain of matter's existence than you or any
other philosopher pretend to be. If there be anything which
makes the generality of mankind averse from the notions I
espouse, it is a misapprehension that I deny the reality of sensible things; but as it is you who are guilty of that and not I,
it follows that in truth their aversion is against your notions
and not mine. I do therefore assert that I am as certain as of
my own being that there are bodies or corporeal substances
(meaning the things I perceive by my senses), and that, granting this, the bulk of mankind will take no thought about, nor
think themselves at all concerned in the fate of, those unknown natures and philosophical quiddities which some men
are so fond of.

Hyl. What say you to this? Since, according to you, men
judge of the reality of things by their senses, how can a man
be mistaken in thinking the moon a plain lucid surface, about
a foot in diameter, or a square tower, seen at a distance, round,
or an oar, with one end in the water, crooked?

Phil. He is not mistaken with regard to the ideas he actually perceives, but in the inferences he makes from his present
perceptions. Thus, in the case of the oar, what he immediately perceives by sight is certainly crooked, and so far he is
in the right. But if he thence conclude that upon taking the
oar out of the water he shall perceive the same crookedness,
or that it would affect his touch as crooked things are wont
to do, in that he is mistaken. In like manner, if he shall conclude, from what he perceives in one station, that, in case he
advances toward the moon or tower, he should still be affected
with the like ideas, he is mistaken. But his mistake lies not
in what he perceives immediately and at present (it being a
manifest contradiction to suppose he should err in respect of
that), but in the wrong judgment he makes concerning the
ideas he apprehends to be connected with those immediately
perceived, or, concerning the ideas, that from what he per-

ceives at present he imagines would be perceived in other circumstances. The case is the same with regard to the Copernican system. We do not here perceive any motion of the earth, but it were erroneous thence to conclude that, in case we were placed at as great a distance from that as we are now from the other planets, we should not then perceive its motion.

Hyl. I understand you and must needs own you say things plausible enough, but give me leave to put you in mind of one thing. Pray, Philonous, were you not formerly as positive that matter existed as you are now that it does not?

Phil. I was. But here lies the difference. Before, my positiveness was founded, without examination, upon prejudice, but now, after inquiry, upon evidence.

Hyl. After all, it seems our dispute is rather about words than things. We agree in the thing, but differ in the name. That we are affected with ideas from without is evident; and it is no less evident that there must be (I will not say archetypes, but) powers without the mind corresponding to those ideas. And as these powers cannot subsist by themselves, there is some subject of them necessarily to be admitted, which I call "matter," and you call "spirit." This is all the difference.

Phil. Pray, Hylas, is that powerful being, or subject of powers, extended?

Hyl. It has not extension, but it has the power to raise in you the idea of extension.

Phil. It is therefore itself unextended?

Hyl. I grant it.

Phil. Is it not also active?

Hyl. Without doubt; otherwise, how could we attribute powers to it?

Phil. Now let me ask you two questions: *First,* whether it be agreeable to the usage either of philosophers or others to give the name "matter" to an unextended active being? And, secondly, whether it be not ridiculously absurd to misapply names contrary to the common use of language?

Hyl. Well then, let it not be called "matter," since you will have it so, but some "third nature," distinct from matter and spirit. For what reason is there why you should call it spirit? Does not the notion of spirit imply that it is thinking as well as active and unextended?

Phil. My reason is this: because I have a mind to have some notion or meaning in what I say, but I have no notion of any action distinct from volition, neither can I conceive volition to be anywhere but in a spirit; therefore, when I speak of an active being I am obliged to mean a spirit. Besides, what can be plainer than that a thing which has no ideas in itself cannot impart them to me; and, if it has ideas, surely it must be a spirit. To make you comprehend the point still more clearly, if it be possible: I assert as well as you that, since we are affected from without, we must allow powers to be without, in a being distinct from ourselves. So far we are agreed. But then we differ as to the kind of this powerful being. I will have it to be spirit, you matter or I know not what (I may add, too, you know not what) third nature. Thus I prove it to be spirit. From the effects I see produced I conclude there are actions; and because actions, volitions; and because there are volitions, there must be a will. Again, the things I perceive must have an existence, they or their archetypes, out of my mind; but, being ideas, neither they nor their achetypes can exist otherwise than in an understanding, there is therefore an understanding. But will and understanding constitute in the strictest sense a mind or spirit. The powerful cause, therefore, of my ideas is in strict propriety of speech a *spirit.*

Hyl. And now I warrant you think you have made the point very clear, little suspecting that what you advance leads directly to a contradiction. Is it not an absurdity to imagine any imperfection in God?

Phil. Without a doubt.

Hyl. To suffer pain is an imperfection?

Phil. It is.

Hyl. Are we not sometimes affected with pain and uneasiness by some other being?

Phil. We are.

Hyl. And have you not said that being is a spirit, and is not that spirit God?

Phil. I grant it.

Hyl. But you have asserted that whatever ideas we perceive from without are in the mind which affects us. The ideas, therefore, of pain and uneasiness are in God, or, in other words, God suffers pain; that is to say, there is an imperfection in the divine nature, which, you acknowledge, was absurd. So you are caught in a plain contradiction.

Phil. That God knows or understands all things, and that He knows, among other things, what pain is, even every sort of painful sensation, and what it is for His creatures to suffer pain, I make no question. But that God, though He knows and sometimes causes painful sensations in us, can Himself suffer pain I positively deny. We, who are limited and dependent spirits, are liable to impressions of sense, the effects of an external agent, which, being produced against our wills, are sometimes painful and uneasy. But God, whom no external being can affect, who perceives nothing by sense as we do, whose will is absolute and independent, causing all things, and liable to be thwarted or resisted by nothing, it is evident such a Being as this can suffer nothing, nor be affected with any painful sensation or, indeed, any sensation at all. We are chained to a body; that is to say, our perceptions are connected with corporeal motions. By the law of our nature we are affected upon every alteration in the nervous parts of our sensible body; which sensible body, rightly considered, is nothing but a complexion of such qualities or ideas as have no existence distinct from being perceived by a mind; so that this connection of sensations with corporeal motions means no more than a correspondence in the order of nature between two sets of ideas, or things immediately perceivable. But God is a pure spirit, disengaged from all such sympathy or natural ties. No corporeal motions are attended with the sensations of pain or pleasure in His mind. To know everything knowable is certainly a perfection, but to endure or suffer or feel anything by sense is an imperfection. The former, I say, agrees to God, but not the latter. God knows or has ideas, but His ideas are not conveyed to Him by sense, as ours are. Your not distinguishing where there is so manifest a difference makes you fancy you see an absurdity where there is none.

Hyl. But all this while you have not considered that the quantity of matter has been demonstrated to be proportional to the gravity of bodies. And what can withstand demonstration?

Phil. Let me see how you demonstrate that point.

Hyl. I lay it down for a principle that the moments or quantities of motion in bodies are in a direct compounded reason of the velocities and quantities of matter contained in them. Hence, where the velocities are equal, it follows the moments are directly as the quantity of matter in each. But it is found by experience that all bodies (bating the small inequalities arising from the resistance of the air) descend with an equal velocity; the motion therefore of descending bodies, and consequently their gravity, which is the cause or principle of that motion, is proportional to the quantity of matter, which was to be demonstrated.

Phil. You lay it down as a self-evident principle that the quantity of motion in any body is proportional to the velocity and matter taken together; and this is made use of to prove a proposition from whence the existence of matter is inferred. Pray is not this arguing in a circle?

Hyl. In the premise I only mean that the motion is proportional to the velocity, jointly with the extension and solidity.

Phil. But allowing this to be true, yet it will not thence follow that gravity is proportional to matter in your philosophic sense of the word, except you take it for granted that unknown *substratum,* or whatever else you call it, is proportional to those sensible qualities which to suppose is plainly begging the question. That there is magnitude and solidity or resistance perceived by sense I readily grant, as likewise, that gravity may be proportional to those qualities I will not dispute. But that either these qualities as perceived by us, or the powers producing them, do exist in a *material substratum*

—this is what I deny, and you, indeed, affirm but, notwithstanding your demonstration, have not yet proved.

Hyl. I shall insist no longer on that point. Do you think, however, you shall persuade me the natural philosophers have been dreaming all this while? Pray what becomes of all their hypotheses and explications of the phenomena which suppose the existence of matter?

Phil. What mean you, Hylas, by the "phenomena"?

Hyl. I mean the appearances which I perceive by my senses.

Phil. And the appearances perceived by sense, are they not ideas?

Hyl. I have told you so a hundred times.

Phil. Therefore, to explain the phenomena is to show how we come to be affected with ideas in that manner and order wherein they are imprinted on our senses. Is it not?

Hyl. It is.

Phil. Now, if you can prove that any philosopher has explained the production of any one idea in our minds by the help of *matter,* I shall forever acquiesce and look on all that has been said against it as nothing; but if you cannot, it is vain to urge the explication of phenomena. That a being endowed with knowledge and will should produce or exhibit ideas is easily understood. But that a being which is utterly destitute of these faculties should be able to produce ideas, or in any sort to affect an intelligence, this I can never understand. This I say, though we had some positive conception of matter, though we knew its qualities and could comprehend its existence, would yet be so far from explaining things that it is itself the most inexplicable thing in the world. And yet, for all this, it will not follow that philosophers have been doing nothing; for by observing and reasoning upon the connection of ideas, they discover the laws and methods of nature, which is a part of knowledge both useful and entertaining.

Hyl. After all, can it be supposed God would deceive all mankind? Do you imagine He would have induced the whole world to believe the being of matter if there was no such thing?

Phil. That every epidemical opinion arising from prejudice, or passion, or thoughtlessness may be imputed to God,
as the Author of it, I believe you will not affirm. Whatsoever
opinion we father on Him, it must be either because He has
discovered it to us by supernatural revelation or because it is
so evident to our natural faculties, which were framed and
given us by God, that it is impossible we should withhold our
assent from it. But where is the revelation? Or where is the
evidence that extorts the belief of matter? Nay, how does it
appear that matter, taken for something distinct from what we
perceive by our senses, is thought to exist by all mankind,
or, indeed, by any except a few philosophers who do not know
what they would be at? Your question supposes these points
are clear; and, when you have cleared them, I shall think myself obliged to give you another answer. In the meantime let
it suffice that I tell you I do not suppose God has deceived
mankind at all.

Hyl. But the novelty, Philonous, the novelty! There lies the
danger. New notions should always be discountenanced; they
unsettle men's minds, and nobody knows where they will end.

Phil. Why the rejecting a notion that has no foundation,
either in sense or in reason or in Divine authority, should be
thought to unsettle the belief of such opinions as are grounded
on all or any of these, I cannot imagine. That innovations in
government and religion are dangerous and ought to be discountenanced, I freely own. But is there the like reason why
they should be discouraged in philosophy? The making anything known which was unknown before is an innovation in
knowledge; and if all such innovations had been forbidden,
men would [not] have made a notable progress in the arts and
sciences. But it is none of my business to plead for novelties
and paradoxes. That the qualities we perceive are not on the
objects, that we must not believe our senses, that we know
nothing of the real nature of things and can never be assured
even of their existence, that real colors and sounds are nothing
but certain unknown figures and motions, that motions are in
themselves neither swift nor slow, that there are in bodies ab-

solute extensions without any particular magnitude or figure, that a thing stupid, thoughtless, and inactive operates on a spirit, that the least particle of a body contains innumerable extended parts—these are the novelties, these are the strange notions which shock the genuine uncorrupted judgment of all mankind, and, being once admitted, embarrass the mind with endless doubts and difficulties. And it is against these and the like innovations I endeavor to vindicate Common Sense. It is true, in doing this I may, perhaps, be obliged to use some ambages and ways of speech not common. But if my notions are once thoroughly understood, that which is most singular in them will, in effect, be found to amount to no more than this—that it is absolutely impossible and a plain contradiction to suppose any unthinking being should exist without being perceived by a mind. And if this notion be singular, it is a shame it should be so at this time of day and in a Christian country.

Hyl. As for the difficulties other opinions may be liable to, those are out of the question. It is your business to defend your own opinion. Can anything be plainer than that you are for changing all things into ideas? You, I say, who are not ashamed to charge me with skepticism. This is so plain, there is no denying it.

Phil. You mistake me. I am not for changing things into ideas but rather ideas into things, since those immediate objects of perception, which, according to you, are only appearances of things, I take to be the real things themselves.

Hyl. Things! you may pretend what you please; but it is certain you leave us nothing but the empty forms of things, the outside only which strikes the senses.

Phil. What you call the empty forms and outside of things seem to me the very things themselves. Nor are they empty or incomplete otherwise than upon your supposition that matter is an essential part of all corporeal things. We both, therefore, agree in this, that we perceive only sensible forms; but herein we differ: you will have them to be empty appearances, I real beings. In short, you do not trust your senses, I do.

Hyl. You say you believe your senses, and seem to applaud yourself that in this you agree with the vulgar. According to you, therefore, the true nature of a thing is discovered by the senses. If so, whence comes that disagreement? Why, is not the same figure, and other sensible qualities, perceived all manner of ways? And why should we use a microscope the better to discover the true nature of a body, if it were discoverable to the naked eye?

Phil. Strictly speaking, Hylas, we do not see the same object that we feel; neither is the same object perceived by the microscope which was by the naked eye. But in case every variation was thought sufficient to constitute a new kind or individual, the endless number or confusion of names would render language impracticable. Therefore, to avoid this as well as other inconveniences which are obvious upon a little thought, men combine together several ideas, apprehended by divers senses, or by the same sense at different times or in different circumstances, but observed, however, to have some connection in nature, either with respect to coexistence or succession; all which they refer to one name and consider as one thing. Hence it follows that when I examine by my other senses a thing I have seen, it is not in order to understand better the same object which I had perceived by sight, the object of one sense not being perceived by the other senses. And when I look through a microscope, it is not that I may perceive more clearly what I perceived already with my bare eyes, the object perceived by the glass being quite different from the former. But in both cases my aim is only to know what ideas are connected together; and the more a man knows of the connection of ideas, the more he is said to know of the nature of things. What, therefore, if our ideas are variable, what if our senses are not in all circumstances affected with the same appearances? It will not thence follow they are not to be trusted or that they are inconsistent either with themselves or anything else, except it be with your preconceived notion of (I know not what) one single, unchanged, unperceivable, real nature, marked by each name; which prejudice seems to have taken its rise from not rightly understanding the common language of men speaking of several distinct ideas as united into one thing by the mind. And, indeed, there is cause to suspect several erroneous conceits of the philosophers are owing to the same original: while they began to build their schemes not so much on notions as words which were framed by the vulgar merely for convenience and dispatch in the common actions of life, without any regard to speculation.

Hyl. Methinks I apprehend your meaning.

Phil. It is your opinion the ideas we perceive by our senses are not real things, but images or copies of them. Our knowledge, therefore, is no further real than as our ideas are the true representations of those originals. But as these supposed originals are in themselves unknown, it is impossible to know how far our ideas resemble them, or whether they resemble them at all. We cannot, therefore, be sure we have any real knowledge. Further, as our ideas are perpetually varied, without any change in the supposed real things, it necessarily follows they cannot all be true copies of them, or, if some are and others are not, it is impossible to distinguish the former from the latter. And this plunges us yet deeper in uncertainty. Again, when we consider the point, we cannot conceive how any idea, or anything like an idea, should have an absolute existence out of a mind, nor consequently, according to you, how there should be any real thing in nature. The result of all which is that we are thrown into the most hopeless and abandoned skepticism. Now give me leave to ask you, *first,* whether your referring ideas to certain absolutely existing unperceived substances, as their originals, be not the source of all this skepticism? *Secondly,* whether you are informed, either by sense or reason, of the existence of those unknown originals? And in case you are not, whether it be not absurd to suppose them? *Thirdly,* whether, upon inquiry, you find there is anything distinctly conceived or meant by the "absolute or external existence of unperceiving substances?" *Lastly,* whether, the premises considered, it be not the wisest way to follow nature, trust your senses, and, laying aside all anxious thought about unknown natures or substances, admit with the vulgar those for real things which are perceived by the senses?

Hyl. For the present I have no inclination to the answering part. I would much rather see how you can get over what follows. Pray, are not the objects perceived by the senses of one likewise perceivable to others present? If there were a hundred more here, they would all see the garden, the trees and flowers, as I see them. But they are not in the same manner affected with the ideas I frame in my imagination. Does not this make a difference between the former sort of objects and the latter?

Phil. I grant it does. Nor have I ever denied a difference between the objects of sense and those of imagination. But what would you infer from thence? You cannot say that sensible objects exist unperceived because they are perceived by many.

Hyl. I own I can make nothing of that objection, but it has led me into another. Is it not your opinion that by our senses we perceive only the ideas existing in our minds?

Phil. It is.

Hyl. But the same idea which is in my mind cannot be in yours or in any other mind. Does it not, therefore, follow from your principles that no two can see the same thing? And is not this highly absurd?

Phil. If the term "same" be taken in the vulgar acceptation, it is certain (and not at all repugnant to the principles I maintain) that different persons may perceive the same thing, or the same thing or idea exist in different minds. Words are of arbitrary imposition; and since men are used to apply the word "same" where no distinction or variety is perceived, and I do not pretend to alter their perceptions, it follows that, as men have said before, *several saw the same thing,* so they may, upon like occasions, still continue to use the same phrase without any deviation either from propriety of language or the truth of things. But if the term "same" be used in the acceptation of philosophers who pretend to an abstracted notion of identity, then, according to their sundry definitions of this notion (for it is not yet agreed wherein that philosophic identity consists), it may or may not be possible for divers persons to perceive the same thing. But whether philosophers shall think fit to call a thing the "same" or no is, I conceive, of small importance. Let us suppose several men together, all endued with the same faculties, and consequently affected in like sort by their senses, and who had yet never known the use of language; they would without question agree in their perceptions. Though perhaps, when they came to the use of speech, some regarding the uniformness of what was perceived might call it the "same" thing; others, especially regarding the diversity of persons who perceived, might choose the denomination of "different" things. But who sees not that all the dispute is about a word, to wit, whether what is perceived by different persons may yet have the term "same" applied to it? Or suppose a house whose walls or outward shell remaining unaltered, the chambers are all pulled down, and new ones built in their place, and that you should call this the "same," and I should say it was not the "same" house—would we not, for all this, perfectly agree in our thoughts of the house considered in itself? And would not all the difference consist in a sound? If you should say we differed in our notions, for that you superadded to your idea of the house the simple abstracted idea of identity, whereas I did not, I would tell you I know not what you mean by that "abstracted idea of identity," and should desire you to look into your own thoughts and be sure you understood yourself.——Why so silent, Hylas? Are you not yet satisfied men may dispute about identity and diversity without any real difference in their thoughts and opinions abstracted from names? Take this further reflection with you—that, whether matter be allowed to exist or no, the case is exactly the same as to the point in hand. For the materialists themselves acknowledge what we immediately perceive by our senses to be our own ideas. Your difficulty, therefore, that no two see the same thing makes equally against the materialists and me.

Hyl. But they suppose an external archetype to which referring their several ideas they may truly be said to perceive the same thing.

Phil. And (not to mention your having discarded those archetypes) so may you suppose an external archetype on my principles; *external,* I mean, to your own mind, though, indeed, it must be supposed to exist in that mind which comprehends all things; but then, this serves all the ends of *identity,* as well as if it existed out of a mind. And I am sure you yourself will not say it is less intelligible.

Hyl. You have indeed clearly satisfied me either that there is no difficulty at bottom in this point or, if there be, that it makes equally against both opinions.

Phil. But that which makes equally against two contradictory opinions can be a proof against neither.

Hyl. I acknowledge it. But, after all, Philonous, when I consider the substance of what you advance against skepticism, it amounts to no more than this: we are sure that we really see, hear, feel, in a word, that we are affected with sensible impressions.

Phil. And how are we concerned any further? I see this cherry, I feel it, I taste it, and I am sure *nothing* cannot be seen or felt or tasted; it is therefore *real.* Take away the sensations of softness, moisture, redness, tartness, and you take away the cherry. Since it is not a being distinct from sensations, a cherry, I say, is nothing but a congeries of sensible impressions, or ideas perceived by various senses, which ideas are united into one thing (or have one name given them) by the mind because they are observed to attend each other. Thus, when the palate is affected with such a particular taste, the sight is affected with a red color, the touch with roundness, softness, etc. Hence, when I see and feel and taste in sundry certain manners, I am sure the cherry exists or is real, its reality being in my opinion nothing abstracted from those sensations. But if by the word "cherry" you mean an unknown nature distinct from all those sensible qualities, and by its "existence" something distinct from its being perceived, then, indeed, I own neither you nor I, nor anyone else, can be sure it exists.

Hyl. But what would you say, Philonous, if I should bring the very same reasons against the existence of sensible things in a mind which you have offered against their existing in a material *substratum?*

Phil. When I see your reasons, you shall hear what I have to say to them.

Hyl. Is the mind extended or unextended?

Phil. Unextended, without doubt.

Hyl. Do you say the things you perceive are in your mind?

Phil. They are.

Hyl. Again, have I not heard you speak of sensible impressions?

Phil. I believe you may.

Hyl. Explain to me now, O Philonous! how is it possible there should be room for all those trees and houses to exist in your mind. Can extended things be contained in that which is unextended? Or are we to imagine impressions made on a thing void of all solidity? You cannot say objects are in your mind, as books in your study, or that things are imprinted on it, as the figure of a seal upon wax. In what sense, therefore, are we to understand those expressions? Explain me this if you can, and I shall then be able to answer all those queries you formerly put to me about my *substratum.*

Phil. Look you, Hylas, when I speak of objects as existing in the mind or imprinted on the senses, I would not be understood in the gross literal sense—as when bodies are said to exist in a place or a seal to make an impression upon wax. My meaning is only that the mind comprehends or perceives them, and that it is affected from without or by some being distinct from itself. This is my explication of your difficulty; and how it can serve to make your tenet of an unperceiving material *substratum* intelligible, I would fain know.

Hyl. Nay, if that be all, I confess I do not see what use can be made of it. But are you not guilty of some abuse of language in this?

Phil. None at all. It is no more than common custom, which you know is the rule of language, has authorized, nothing be-

ing more usual than for philosophers to speak of the immediate objects of the understanding as things existing in the
mind. Nor is there anything in this but what is conformable
to the general analogy of language; most part of the mental
operations being signified by words borrowed from sensible
things, as is plain in the terms "comprehend," "reflect," "discourse," etc., which, being applied to the mind, must not be
taken in their gross original sense.

Hyl. You have, I own, satisfied me in this point. But there
still remains one great difficulty which I know not how you
will get over. And, indeed, it is of such importance that if
you could solve all others without being able to find a solution for this, you must never expect to make me a proselyte to
your principles.

Phil. Let me know this mighty difficulty.

Hyl. The Scripture account of the creation is what appears
to me utterly irreconcilable with your notions. Moses tells us
of a creation—a creation of what? of ideas? No, certainly, but
of things, of real things, solid corporeal substances. Bring your
principles to agree with this and I shall perhaps agree with
you.

Phil. Moses mentions the sun, moon, and stars, earth and
sea, plants and animals. That all these do really exist and
were in the beginning created by God, I make no question.
If by "ideas" you mean fictions and fancies of the mind, then
these are no ideas. If by "ideas" you mean immediate objects of the understanding, or sensible things which cannot
exist unperceived, or out of a mind, then these things are
ideas. But whether you do or do not call them "ideas," it matters little. The difference is only about a name. And whether
that name be retained or rejected, the sense, the truth, and
reality of things continues the same. In common talk, the objects of our senses are not termed "ideas" but "things." Call
them so still, provided you do not attribute to them any absolute external existence, and I shall never quarrel with you for
a word. The creation, therefore, I allow to have been a creation of things, of *real* things. Neither is this in the least in-

consistent with my principles, as is evident from what I have now said; and would have been evident to you without this if you had not forgotten what had been so often said before. But as for solid corporeal substances, I desire you to show where Moses makes any mention of them; and if they should be mentioned by him or any other inspired writer, it would still be incumbent on you to show those words were not taken in the vulgar acceptation for things falling under our senses, but in the philosophic acceptation for matter or an unknown quiddity with an absolute existence. When you have proved these points, then (and not till then) may you bring the authority of Moses into our dispute.

Hyl. It is in vain to dispute about a point so clear. I am content to refer it to your own conscience. Are you not satisfied there is some peculiar repugnancy between the Mosaic account of the creation and your notions?

Phil. If all possible sense which can be put on the first chapter of Genesis may be conceived as consistently with my principles as any other, then it has no peculiar repugnancy with them. But there is no sense you may not as well conceive, believing as I do. Since, besides spirits, all you conceive are ideas, and the existence of these I do not deny. Neither do you pretend they exist without the mind.

Hyl. Pray let me see any sense you can understand it in.

Phil. Why, I imagine that if I had been present at the creation, I should have seen things produced into being—that is become perceptible—in the order prescribed by the sacred historian. I ever before believed the Mosaic account of the creation, and now find no alteration in my manner of believing it. When things are said to begin or end their existence, we do not mean this with regard to God, but His creatures. All objects are eternally known by God, or, which is the same thing, have an eternal existence in His mind; but when things, before imperceptible to creatures, are, by a decree of God, made perceptible to them, then are they said to begin a relative existence with respect to created minds. Upon reading therefore the Mosaic account of the creation, I understand that the several parts of the world became gradually perceivable to finite spirits endowed with proper faculties, so that, whoever such were present, they were in truth perceived by them. This is the literal obvious sense suggested to me by the words of the Holy Scripture, in which is included no mention or thought either of *substratum,* instrument, occasion, or absolute existence. And, upon inquiry, I doubt not it will be found that most plain honest men who believe the creation never think of those things any more than I. What metaphysical sense you may understand it in, you only can tell.

Hyl. But, Philonous, you do not seem to be aware that you allow created things in the beginning only a relative and consequently hypothetical being; that is to say, upon supposition there were men to perceive them, without which they have no actuality of absolute existence wherein creation might terminate. Is it not, therefore, according to you, plainly impossible the creation of any inanimate creatures should precede that of man? And is not this directly contrary to the Mosaic account?

Phil. In answer to that, I say, *first,* created beings might begin to exist in the mind of other created intelligences besides men. You will not, therefore, be able to prove any contradiction between Moses and my notions unless you first show there was no other order of finite created spirits in being before man. I say further, in case we conceive the creation as we should at this time a parcel of plants or vegetables of all sorts produced by an invisible power in a desert where nobody was present—that this way of explaining or conceiving it is consistent with my principles, since they deprive you of nothing, either sensible or imaginable; that it exactly suits with the common, natural, and undebauched notions of mankind; that it manifests the dependence of all things on God, and consequently has all the good effect or influence, which it is possible that important article of our faith should have in making men humble, thankful, and resigned to their Creator. I say, moreover, that, in this naked conception of things, divested of words, there will not be found any notion of what you call the "actuality of absolute existence." You may indeed raise a dust with those terms and so lengthen our dispute to no purpose. But I entreat you calmly to look into your own thoughts and then tell me if they are not a useless and unintelligible jargon.

Hyl. I own I have no very clear notion annexed to them. But what say you to this? Do you not make the existence of sensible things consist in their being in a mind? And were not all things externally in the mind of God? Did they not therefore exist from all eternity, according to you? And how could that which was eternal be created in time? Can anything be clearer or better connected than this?

Phil. And are not you too of opinion that God knew all things from eternity?

Hyl. I am.

Phil. Consequently, they always had a being in the Divine intellect.

Hyl. This I acknowledge.

Phil. By your own confession, therefore, nothing is new, or begins to be, in respect of the mind of God. So we are agreed in that point.

Hyl. What shall we make then of the creation?

Phil. May we not understand it to have been entirely in respect of finite spirits, so that things, with regard to us, may properly be said to begin their existence, or be created, when God decreed they should become perceptible to intelligent creatures in that order and manner which He then established and we now call the laws of nature? You may call this a "relative," or "hypothetical existence," if you please. But so long as it supplies us with the most natural, obvious, and literal sense of the Mosaic history of the creation, so long as it answers all the religious ends of that great article, in a word, so long as you can assign no other sense or meaning in its stead, why should we reject this? Is it to comply with a ridiculous skeptical humor of making everything nonsense and unintelligible? I am sure you cannot say it is for the glory of God. For allowing it to be a thing possible and conceivable that the corporeal world should have an absolute existence extrinsical to the mind of God, as well as to the minds of all created spirits, yet how could this set forth either the immensity or omniscience of the Deity or the necessary and immediate dependence of all things on Him? Nay, would it not rather seem to derogate from those attributes?

Hyl. Well, but as to this decree of God's for making things perceptible, what say you, Philonous, is it not plain God did either execute that decree from all eternity or at some certain time began to will what He had not actually willed before, but only designed to will? If the former, then there could be no creation or beginning of existence in finite things. If the latter, then we must acknowledge something new to befall the Deity, which implies a sort of change; and all change argues imperfection.

Phil. Pray consider what you are doing. Is it not evident this objection concludes equally against a creation in any sense, nay, against every other act of the Deity discoverable by the light of nature? None of which can we conceive otherwise than as performed in time and having a beginning. God is a Being of transcendent and unlimited perfections; His Nature, therefore, is incomprehensible to finite spirits. It is not, therefore, to be expected that any man, whether *materialist* or *immaterialist,* should have exactly just notions of the Deity, His attributes, and ways of operation. If then you would infer anything against me, your difficulty must not be drawn from the inadequateness of our conceptions of the Divine nature, which is unavoidable on any scheme, but from the denial of matter, of which there is not one word, directly or indirectly, in what you have now objected.

Hyl. I must acknowledge the difficulties you are concerned to clear are such only as arise from the nonexistence of matter and are peculiar to that notion. So far you are in the right. But I cannot by any means bring myself to think there is no such peculiar repugnancy between the creation and your opinion, though, indeed, where to fix it I do not distinctly know.

Phil. What would you have? Do I not acknowledge a two-

fold state of things, the one ectypal or natural, the other arche-
typal and eternal? The former was created in time, the latter
existed from everlasting in the mind of God. Is not this agreeable to the common notions of divines? Or is any more than
this necessary in order to conceive the creation? But you suspect some peculiar repugnancy, though you know not where
it lies. To take away all possibility of scruple in the case, do
but consider this one point: either you are not able to conceive the creation on any hypothesis whatsoever, and if so,
there is no ground for dislike or complaint against my particular opinion on that score; or you are able to conceive it,
and if so, why not on my principles, since thereby nothing
conceivable is taken away? You have all along been allowed
the full scope of sense, imagination, and reason. Whatever,
therefore, you could before apprehend, either immediately or
mediately by your senses, or by ratiocination from your senses,
whatever you could perceive, imagine, or understand, remains
still with you. If, therefore, the notion you have of the creation
by other principles be intelligible, you have it still upon mine;
if it be not intelligible, I conceive it to be no notion at all,
and so there is no loss of it. And, indeed, it seems to me very
plain that the supposition of matter, that is, a thing perfectly
unknown and inconceivable, cannot serve to make us conceive anything. And I hope it need not be proved to you that
if the existence of matter does not make the creation conceivable, the creation's being without it inconceivable can be no
objection against its nonexistence.

Hyl. I confess, Philonous, you have almost satisfied me in
this point of the creation.

Phil. I would fain know why you are not quite satisfied.
You tell me indeed of a repugnancy between the Mosaic history and immaterialism, but you know not where it lies. Is
this reasonable, Hylas? Can you expect I should solve a difficulty without knowing what it is? But, to pass by all that,
would not a man think you were assured there is no repugnancy between the received notions of materialists and the
inspired writings?

Hyl. And so I am.

Phil. Ought the historical part of Scripture to be understood in a plain obvious sense or in a sense which is metaphysical and out of the way?

Hyl. In the plain sense, doubtless.

Phil. When Moses speaks of herbs, earth, water, etc. as having been created by God, think you not the sensible things commonly signified by those words are suggested to every unphilosophical reader?

Hyl. I cannot help thinking so.

Phil. And are not all ideas, or things perceived by sense, to be denied a real existence by the doctrine of the materialists?

Hyl. This I have already acknowledged.

Phil. The creation, therefore, according to them, was not the creation of things sensible, which have only a relative being, but of certain unknown natures which have an absolute being wherein creation might terminate?

Hyl. True.

Phil. Is it not, therefore, evident the assertors of matter destroy the plain obvious sense of Moses, with which their notions are utterly inconsistent, and instead of it obtrude on us I know not what, something equally unintelligible to themselves and me?

Hyl. I cannot contradict you.

Phil. Moses tells us of a creation. A creation of what? of unknown quiddities, of occasions, or *substratum?* No, certainly, but of things obvious to the senses. You must first reconcile this with your notions if you expect I should be reconciled to them.

Hyl. I see you can assault me with my own weapons.

Phil. Then as to *absolute existence,* was there ever known a more jejune notion than that? Something it is so abstracted and unintelligible that you have frankly owned you could not conceive it, much less explain anything by it. But allowing matter to exist and the notion of absolute existence to be as clear as light, yet, was this ever known to make the creation more credible? Nay, has it not furnished the atheists and infidels of all ages with the most plausible arguments against a creation? That a corporeal substance which has an absolute existence without the minds of spirits should be produced out of nothing, by the mere will of a spirit, has been looked upon as a thing so contrary to all reason, so impossible and absurd, that not only the most celebrated among the ancients, but even divers modern and Christian philosophers have thought matter co-eternal with the Deity. Lay these things together and then judge you whether materialism disposes men to believe the creation of things.

Hyl. I own, Philonous, I think it does not. This of the creation is the last objection I can think of; and I must needs own it has been sufficiently answered as well as the rest. Nothing now remains to be overcome but a sort of unaccountable backwardness that I find in myself toward your notions.

Phil. When a man is swayed, he knows not why, to one side of a question, can this, think you, be anything else but the effect of prejudice, which never fails to attend old and rooted notions? And, indeed, in this respect I cannot deny the belief of matter to have very much the advantage over the contrary opinion with men of a learned education.

Hyl. I confess it seems to be as you say.

Phil. As a balance, therefore, to this weight of prejudice, let us throw into the scale the great advantages that arise from the belief of immaterialism, both in regard to religion and human learning. The being of a God and incorruptibility of the soul, those great articles of religion, are they not proved with the clearest and most immediate evidence? When I say the being of a *God,* I do not mean an obscure general cause of things whereof we have no conception, but *God* in the strict and proper sense of the word, a Being whose spirituality, omnipresence, providence, omniscience, infinite power, and goodness are as conspicuous as the existence of sensible things, of which (notwithstanding the fallacious pretenses and affected scruples of skeptics) there is no more reason to doubt than of our own being. Then, with relation to human sciences: in Natural Philosophy, what intricacies, what obscurities, what

contradictions has the belief of matter led men into! To say
nothing of the numberless disputes about its extent, contin-
uity, homogeneity, gravity, divisibility, etc.—do they not pretend to explain all things by bodies operating on bodies, according to the laws of motion? And yet, are they able to comprehend how any one body should move another? Nay, admitting there was no difficulty in reconciling the notion of an
inert being with a cause, or in conceiving how an accident
might pass from one body to another, yet, by all their strained
thoughts and extravagant suppositions, have they been able to
reach the mechanical production of any one animal or vegetable body? Can they account, by the laws of motion, for
sounds, tastes, smells, or colors, or for the regular course of
things? Have they accounted, by physical principles, for the
aptitude and contrivance even of the most inconsiderable parts
of the universe? But laying aside matter and corporeal causes
and admitting only the efficiency of an All-perfect Mind, are
not all the effects of nature easy and intelligible? If the *phenomena* are nothing else but *ideas,* God is a *spirit,* but matter
an unintelligent, unperceiving being. If they demonstrate an
unlimited power in their cause, God is active and omnipotent,
but matter an inert mass. If the order, regularity, and usefulness of them can never be sufficiently admired, God is infinitely
wise and provident, but matter destitute of all contrivance
and design. These surely are great advantages in physics. Not
to mention that the apprehension of a distant Deity naturally
disposes men to a negligence of their moral actions, which they
would be more cautious of, in case they thought him immediately present and acting on their minds without the interposi-
tion of matter or unthinking second causes. Then in metaphysics: what difficulties concerning entity in abstract, substan-
tial forms, hylarchic principles, plastic natures, substance and
accident, principle of individuation, possibility of matter's
thinking, origin of ideas, the manner how two independent
substances so widely different as *spirit* and *matter* should mutually operate on each other? What difficulties, I say, and endless
disquisitions concerning these and innumerable other the like

points do we escape by supposing only spirits and ideas? Even the mathematics themselves, if we take away the absolute existence of extended things, become much more clear and easy, the most shocking paradoxes and intricate speculations in those sciences depending on the infinite divisibility of finite extension, which depends on that supposition. But what need is there to insist on the particular sciences? Is not that opposition to all science whatsoever, that frenzy of the ancient and modern skeptics, built on the same foundation? Or can you produce so much as one argument against the reality of corporeal things or in behalf of that avowed utter ignorance of their natures which does not suppose their reality to consist in an external absolute existence? Upon this supposition, indeed, the objections from the change of colors in a pigeon's neck, or the appearance of the broken oar in the water, must be allowed to have weight. But these and the like objections vanish if we do not maintain the being of absolute external originals, but place the reality of things in ideas, fleeting, indeed, and changeable; however, not changed at random, but according to the fixed order of nature. For herein consists that constancy and truth of things which secures all the concerns of life, and distinguishes that which is real from the irregular visions of the fancy.

Hyl. I agree to all you have now said and must own that nothing can incline me to embrace your opinion more than the advantages I see it is attended with. I am by nature lazy, and this would be a mighty abridgment in knowledge. What doubts, what hypotheses, what labyrinths of amusement, what fields of disputation, what an ocean of false learning may be avoided by that single notion of *immaterialism!*

Phil. After all, is there anything further remaining to be done? You may remember you promised to embrace that opinion which upon examination should appear most agreeable to common sense and remote from skepticism. This, by your own confession, is that which denies matter or the absolute existence of corporeal things. Nor is this all; the same notion has been proved several ways, viewed in different lights, pursued in its consequences, and all objections against it cleared. Can there be a greater evidence of its truth? Or is it possible it should have all the marks of a true opinion and yet be false?

Hyl. I own myself entirely satisfied for the present in all respects. But what security can I have that I shall still continue the same full assent to your opinion and that no unthought-of objection or difficulty will occur hereafter?

Phil. Pray, Hylas, do you in other cases, when a point is once evidently proved, withhold your assent on account of objections or difficulties it may be liable to? Are the difficulties that attend the doctrine of incommensurable quantities, of the angle of contact, of the asymptotes to curves, or the like, sufficient to make you hold out against mathematical demonstration? Or will you disbelieve the Providence of God because there may be some particular things which you know not how to reconcile with it? If there are difficulties attending immaterialism, there are at the same time direct and evident proofs of it. But for the existence of matter there is not one proof, and far more numerous and insurmountable objections lie against it. But where are those mighty difficulties you insist on? Alas! you know not where or what they are; something which may possibly occur hereafter. If this be a sufficient pretense for withholding your full assent, you should never yield it to any proposition, how free soever from exceptions, how clearly and solidly soever demonstrated.

Hyl. You have satisfied me, Philonous.

Phil. But to arm you against all future objections, do but consider that which bears equally hard on two contradictory opinions can be proof against neither. Whenever, therefore, any difficulty occurs, try if you can find a solution for it on the hypothesis of the materialists. Be not deceived by words, but sound your own thoughts. And in case you cannot conceive it easier by the help of materialism, it is plain it can be no objection against immaterialism. Had you proceeded all along by this rule, you would probably have spared yourself abundance of trouble in objecting, since of all your difficulties I challenge you to show one that is explained by matter, nay, which is not more unintelligible with than without that supposition, and consequently makes rather *against* than *for* it. You should consider, in each particular, whether the difficulty arises from the *nonexistence of matter*. If it does not, you might as well argue from the infinite divisibility of extension against the Divine prescience as from such a difficulty against immaterialism. And yet, upon recollection, I believe you will find this to have been often if not always the case. You should likewise take heed not to argue on a *petitio principii*. One is apt to say the unknown substances ought to be esteemed real things rather than the ideas in our minds; and who can tell but the unthinking external substance may concur as a cause or instrument in the productions of our ideas? But is not this proceeding on a supposition that there are such external substances? And to suppose this, is it not begging the question? But above all things, you should beware of imposing on yourself by that vulgar sophism which is called *ignoratio elenchi*. You talked often as if you thought I maintained the nonexistence of sensible things, whereas in truth no one can be more thoroughly assured of their existence than I am; and it is you who doubt, I should have said, positively deny it. Everything that is seen, felt, heard, or any way perceived by the senses is, on the principles I embrace, a real being, but not on yours. Remember, the matter you contend for is an unknown somewhat (if indeed it may be termed "somewhat"), which is quite stripped of all sensible qualities, and can neither be perceived by sense, nor apprehended by the mind. Remember, I say that it is not any object which is hard or soft, hot or cold, blue or white, round or square, etc.—for all these things I affirm do exist. Though, indeed, I deny they have an existence distinct from being perceived, or that they exist out of all minds whatsoever. Think on these points; let them be attentively considered and still kept in view. Otherwise you will not comprehend the state of the question, without which your objections will always be wide of the mark and, instead of mine, may possibly be directed (as more than once they have been) against your own notions.

Hyl. I must needs own, Philonous, nothing seems to have kept me from agreeing with you more than this same *mistaking the question.* In denying matter, at first glimpse I am tempted to imagine you deny the things we see and feel, but, upon reflection, find there is no ground for it. What think you, therefore, of retaining the name "matter" and applying it to *sensible things?* This may be done without any change in your sentiments; and, believe me, it would be a means of reconciling them to some persons who may be more shocked at an innovation in words than in opinion.

Phil. With all my heart; retain the word "matter" and apply it to the objects of sense, if you please, provided you do not attribute to them any subsistence distinct from their being perceived. I shall never quarrel with you for an expression. "Matter" or "material substance" are terms introduced by philosophers, and, as used by them, imply a sort of independence, or a subsistence distinct from being perceived by a mind; but are never used by common people, or, if ever, it is to signify the immediate objects of sense. One would think, therefore, so long as the names of all particular things with the terms "sensible," "substance," "body," "stuff," and the like, are retained, the word "matter" should be never missed in common talk. And in philosophical discourses it seems the best way to leave it quite out, since there is not, perhaps, any one thing that has more favored and strengthened the depraved bent of the mind toward atheism than the use of that general confused term.

Hyl. Well, but, Philonous, since I am content to give up the notion of an unthinking substance exterior to the mind, I think you ought not to deny me the privilege of using the word "matter" as I please, and annexing it to a collection of sensible qualities subsisting only in the mind. I freely own there is no other substance, in a strict sense, than spirit. But I have been so long accustomed to the term "matter" that I know not how to part with it. To say there is no matter in the world is still shocking to me. Whereas to say there is no matter if by that term be meant an unthinking substance existing without the mind, but if by matter is meant some sensible thing whose existence consists in being perceived, then there is matter—this distinction gives it quite another turn; and men will come into your notions with small difficulty when they are proposed in that manner. For, after all, the controversy about matter in the strict acceptation of it lies altogether between you and the philosophers, whose principles, I acknowledge, are not near so natural or so agreeable to the common sense of mankind and Holy Scripture as yours. There is nothing we either desire or shun but as it makes, or is apprehended to make, some part of our happiness or misery. But what has happiness or misery, joy or grief, pleasure or pain to do with absolute existence or with unknown entities abstracted from all relation to us? It is evident things regard us only as they are pleasing or displeasing; and they can please or displease only so far forth as they are perceived. Further, therefore, we are not concerned; and thus far you leave things as you found them. Yet still there is something new in this doctrine. It is plain, I do not now think with the philosophers, nor yet altogether with the vulgar. I would know how the case stands in that respect, precisely what you have added to or altered in my former notions.

Phil. I do not pretend to be a setter-up of new notions. My endeavors tend only to unite and place in a clearer light that truth which was before shared between the vulgar and the philosophers, the former being of opinion that *those things they immediately perceive are the real things,* and the latter, that *the things immediately perceived are ideas which exist only in the mind.* Which two notions put together do, in effect, constitute the substance of what I advance.

Hyl. I have been a long time distrusting my senses; methought I saw things by a dim light and through false glasses. Now the glasses are removed and a new light breaks in upon my understanding. I am clearly convinced that I see things in their native forms and am no longer in pain about their *unknown natures* or *absolute existence.* This is the state I find myself in at present, though, indeed, the course that brought me to it I do not yet thoroughly comprehend. You set out upon the same principles that Academics, Cartesians, and the like sects usually do, and for a long time it looked as if you were advancing their philosophical skepticism; but, in the end, your conclusions are directly opposite to theirs.

Phil. You see, Hylas, the water of yonder fountain, how it is forced upwards, in a round column, to a certain height, at which it breaks and falls back into the basin from whence it rose, its ascent as well as descent proceeding from the same uniform law or principle of gravitation. Just so, the same principles which, at first view, lead to skepticism, pursued to a certain point, bring men back to common sense.